SILK TAPESTRY
AND OTHER CHINESE FOLKTALES

Songs of Our Ancestors
Volume II

PATRICK ATANGAN

NANTIER · BEALL · MINOUSTCHINE

Also available:
Songs of Our Ancestors, vol. 1:
The Yellow Jar: $12.95

($3 P&H 1st item, $1 each addt'l)

We have over 200 graphic
novels in print, write
for our color catalog:
NBM, dept. S
555 8th Ave., Suite 1202
New York, NY 10018
www.nbmpublishing.com
www.atangan.com

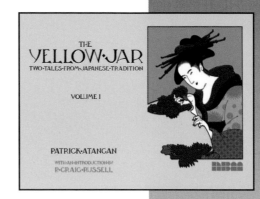

ISBN 1-56163-403-4
© 2004 Patrick Atangan
Printed in China

5   4   3   2   1

                    Library of Congress Cataloging-in-Publication Data

Atangan, Patrick.
    The silk tapestry and other Chinese folktales / Patrick Atangan.
        p.cm.-- (Songs of our ancestors ; 2)
    ISBN 1-56163-403-4 (alk. paper)
        I. Title. II. Series.

PN6727.A87S56 2004
741.5'973--dc22

                                    2004049990

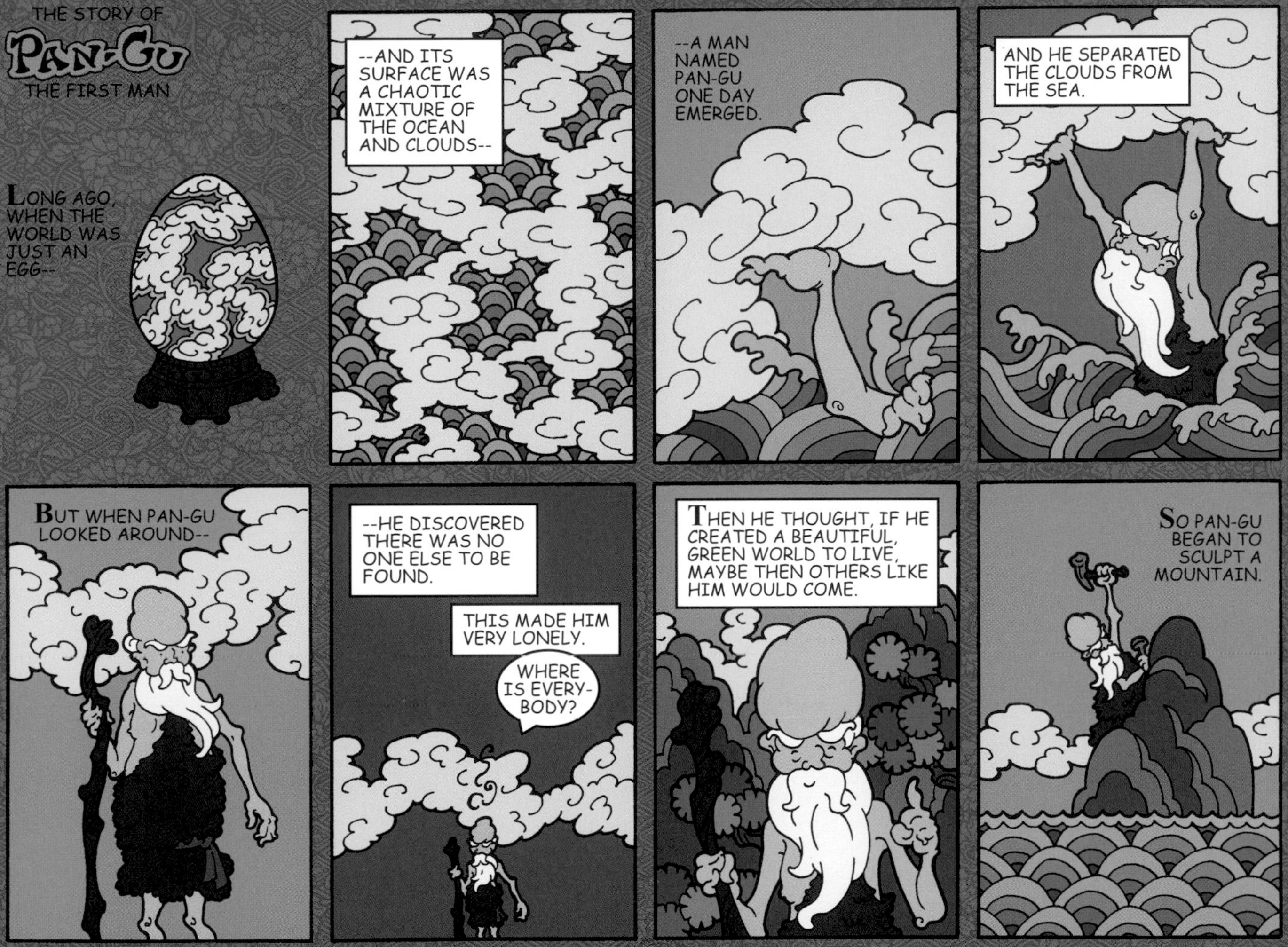
THE STORY OF
PAN-GU
THE FIRST MAN
LONG AGO, WHEN THE WORLD WAS JUST AN EGG--
--AND ITS SURFACE WAS A CHAOTIC MIXTURE OF THE OCEAN AND CLOUDS--
--A MAN NAMED PAN-GU ONE DAY EMERGED.
AND HE SEPARATED THE CLOUDS FROM THE SEA.
BUT WHEN PAN-GU LOOKED AROUND--
--HE DISCOVERED THERE WAS NO ONE ELSE TO BE FOUND.
THIS MADE HIM VERY LONELY.
WHERE IS EVERY-BODY?
THEN HE THOUGHT, IF HE CREATED A BEAUTIFUL, GREEN WORLD TO LIVE, MAYBE THEN OTHERS LIKE HIM WOULD COME.
SO PAN-GU BEGAN TO SCULPT A MOUNTAIN.

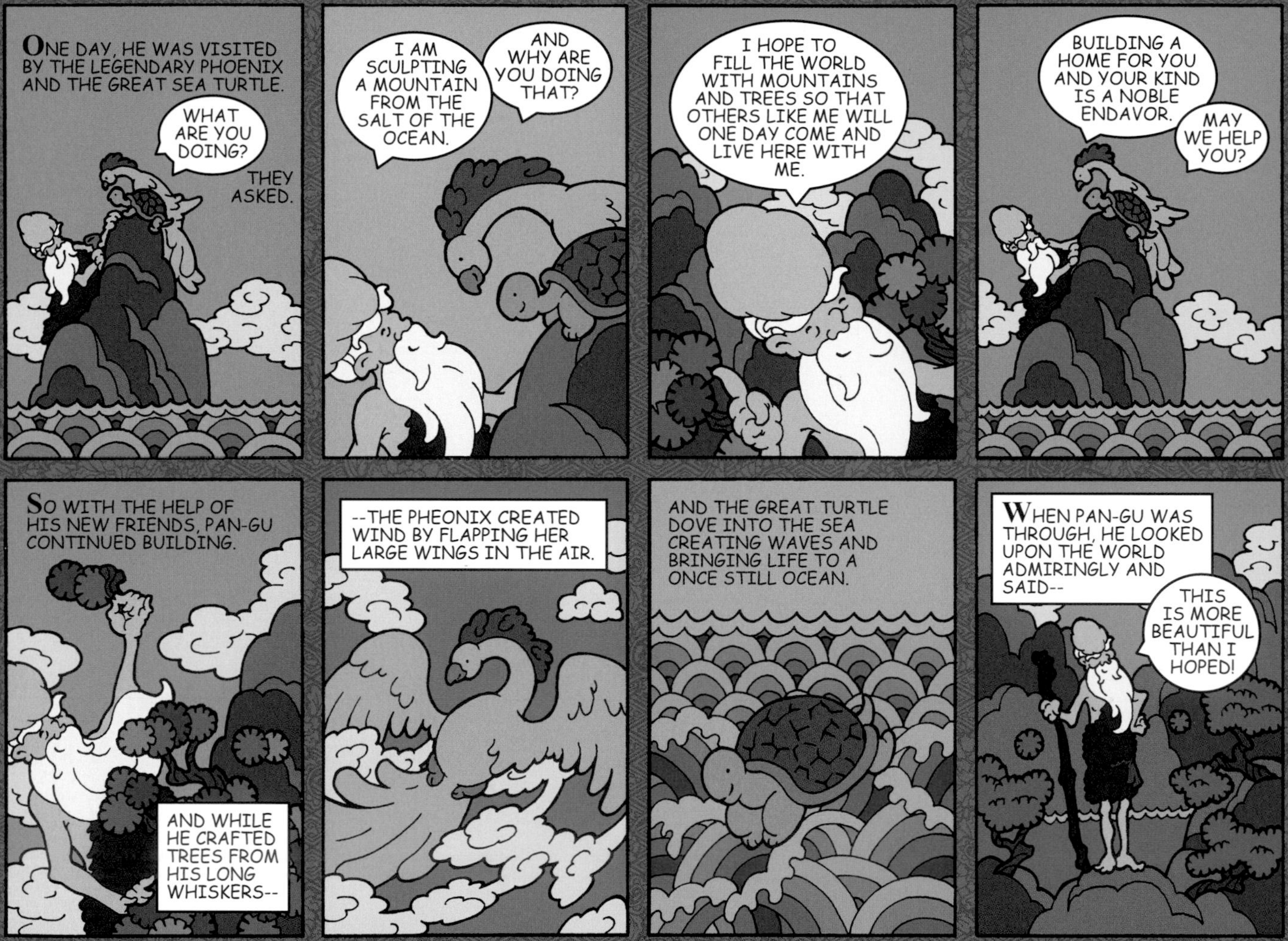

ONE DAY, HE WAS VISITED BY THE LEGENDARY PHOENIX AND THE GREAT SEA TURTLE.
WHAT ARE YOU DOING?
THEY ASKED.
I AM SCULPTING A MOUNTAIN FROM THE SALT OF THE OCEAN.
AND WHY ARE YOU DOING THAT?
I HOPE TO FILL THE WORLD WITH MOUNTAINS AND TREES SO THAT OTHERS LIKE ME WILL ONE DAY COME AND LIVE HERE WITH ME.
BUILDING A HOME FOR YOU AND YOUR KIND IS A NOBLE ENDAVOR.
MAY WE HELP YOU?
SO WITH THE HELP OF HIS NEW FRIENDS, PAN-GU CONTINUED BUILDING.
AND WHILE HE CRAFTED TREES FROM HIS LONG WHISKERS--
--THE PHEONIX CREATED WIND BY FLAPPING HER LARGE WINGS IN THE AIR.
AND THE GREAT TURTLE DOVE INTO THE SEA CREATING WAVES AND BRINGING LIFE TO A ONCE STILL OCEAN.
WHEN PAN-GU WAS THROUGH, HE LOOKED UPON THE WORLD ADMIRINGLY AND SAID--
THIS IS MORE BEAUTIFUL THAN I HOPED!

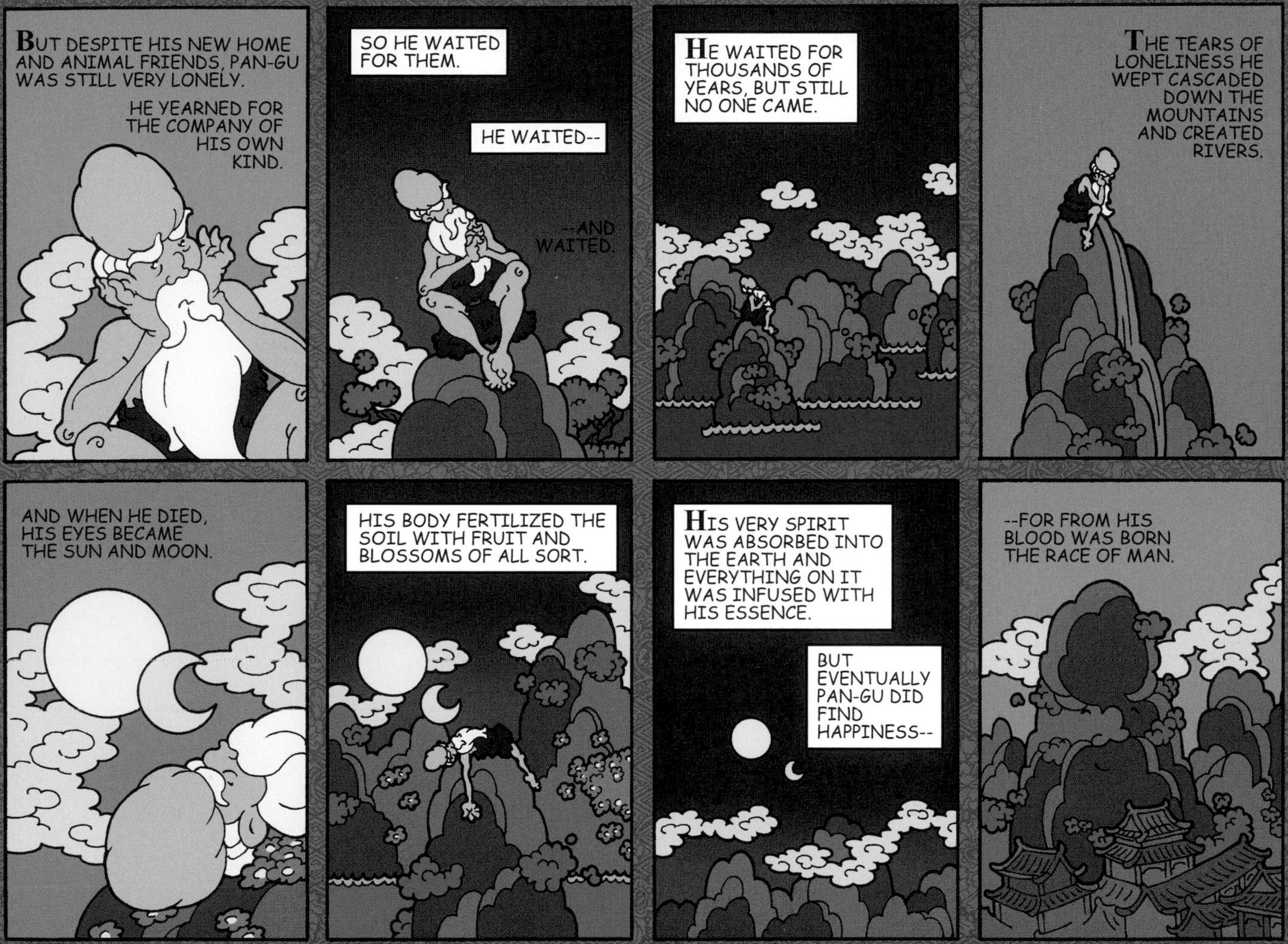
BUT DESPITE HIS NEW HOME AND ANIMAL FRIENDS, PAN-GU WAS STILL VERY LONELY.
HE YEARNED FOR THE COMPANY OF HIS OWN KIND.
SO HE WAITED FOR THEM.
HE WAITED--
--AND WAITED.
HE WAITED FOR THOUSANDS OF YEARS, BUT STILL NO ONE CAME.
THE TEARS OF LONELINESS HE WEPT CASCADED DOWN THE MOUNTAINS AND CREATED RIVERS.
AND WHEN HE DIED, HIS EYES BECAME THE SUN AND MOON.
HIS BODY FERTILIZED THE SOIL WITH FRUIT AND BLOSSOMS OF ALL SORT.
HIS VERY SPIRIT WAS ABSORBED INTO THE EARTH AND EVERYTHING ON IT WAS INFUSED WITH HIS ESSENCE.
BUT EVENTUALLY PAN-GU DID FIND HAPPINESS--
--FOR FROM HIS BLOOD WAS BORN THE RACE OF MAN.

THE END

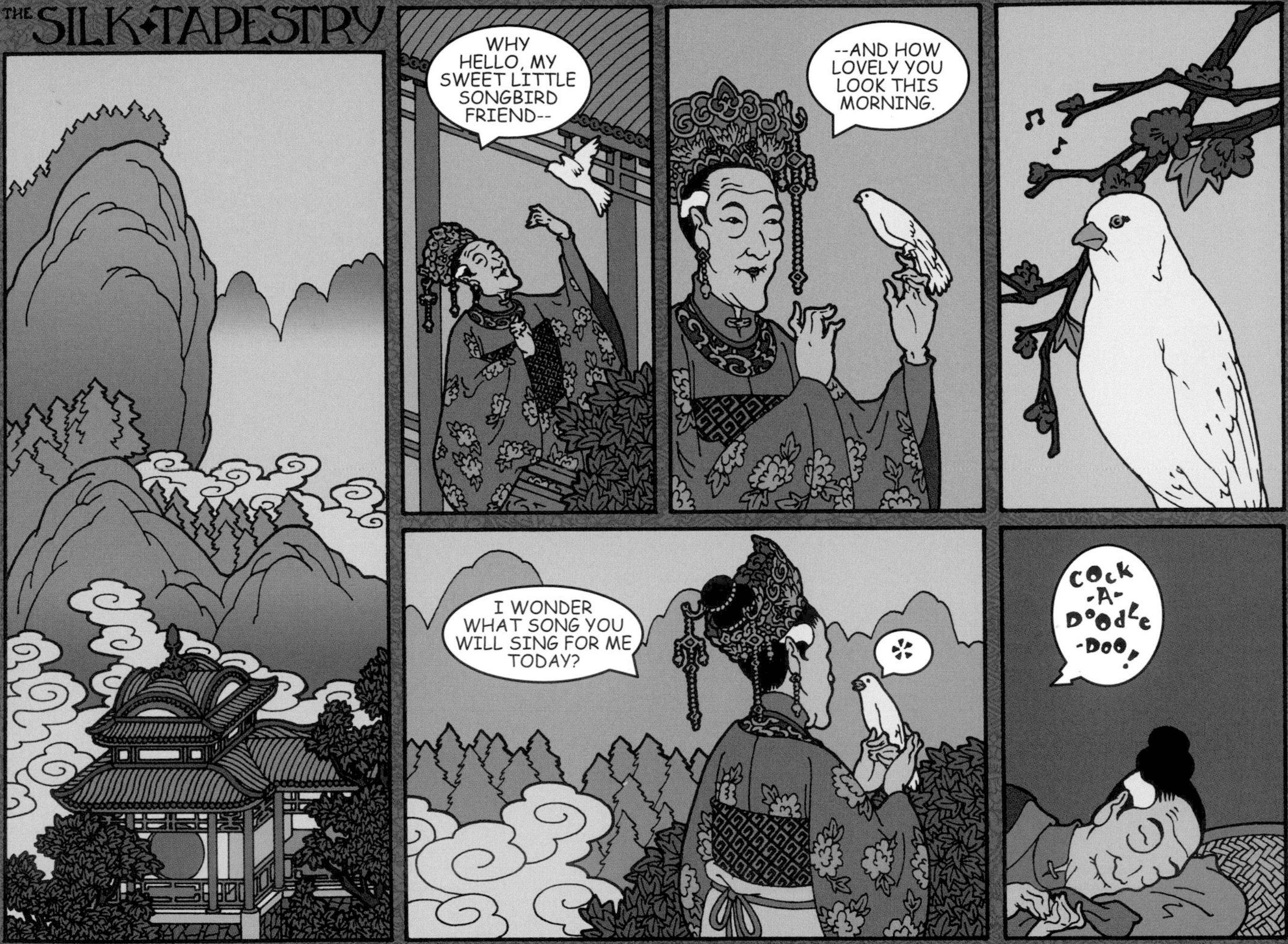
WHY HELLO, MY SWEET LITTLE SONGBIRD FRIEND--
--AND HOW LOVELY YOU LOOK THIS MORNING.
I WONDER WHAT SONG YOU WILL SING FOR ME TODAY?
COCK-A-DOODLE-DOO!

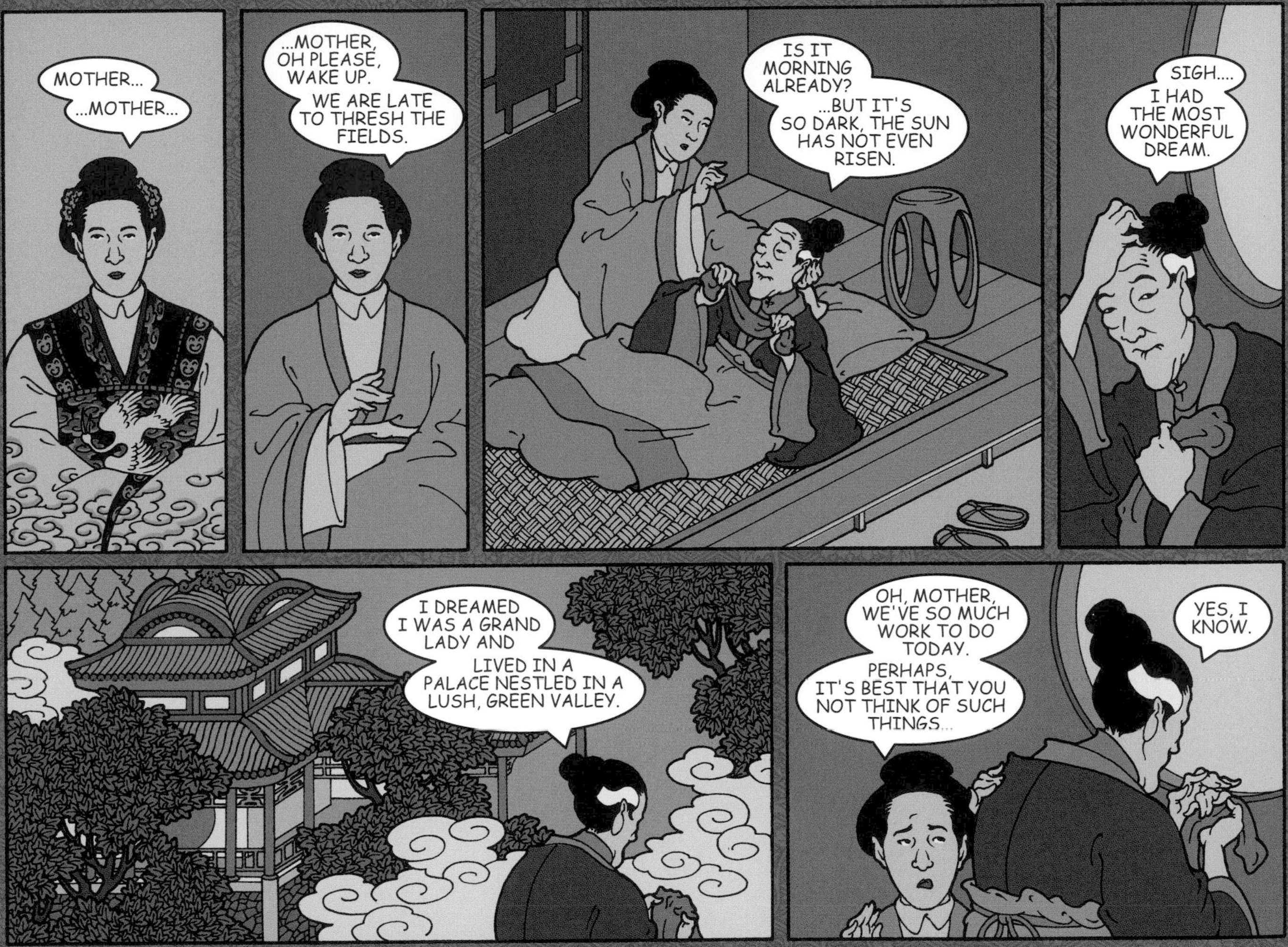

MOTHER...
...MOTHER...
...MOTHER, OH PLEASE, WAKE UP.
WE ARE LATE TO THRESH THE FIELDS.
IS IT MORNING ALREADY?
...BUT IT'S SO DARK, THE SUN HAS NOT EVEN RISEN.
SIGH....
I HAD THE MOST WONDERFUL DREAM.
I DREAMED I WAS A GRAND LADY AND
LIVED IN A PALACE NESTLED IN A LUSH, GREEN VALLEY.
OH, MOTHER, WE'VE SO MUCH WORK TO DO TODAY.
PERHAPS, IT'S BEST THAT YOU NOT THINK OF SUCH THINGS...
YES, I KNOW.

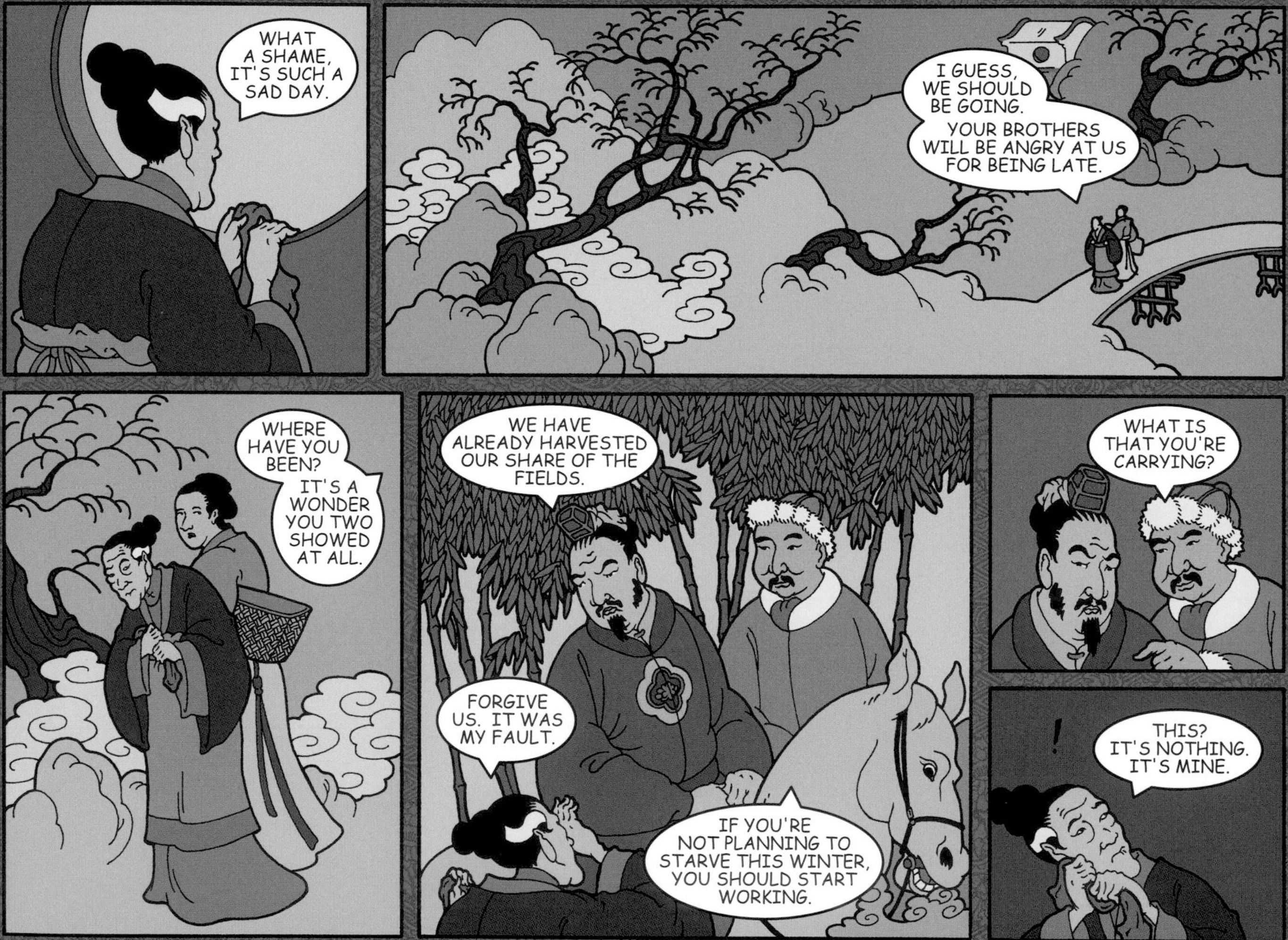
WHAT A SHAME, IT'S SUCH A SAD DAY.
I GUESS, WE SHOULD BE GOING.
YOUR BROTHERS WILL BE ANGRY AT US FOR BEING LATE.
WHERE HAVE YOU BEEN?
IT'S A WONDER YOU TWO SHOWED AT ALL.
WE HAVE ALREADY HARVESTED OUR SHARE OF THE FIELDS.
FORGIVE US. IT WAS MY FAULT.
IF YOU'RE NOT PLANNING TO STARVE THIS WINTER, YOU SHOULD START WORKING.
WHAT IS THAT YOU'RE CARRYING?
!
THIS? IT'S NOTHING. IT'S MINE.

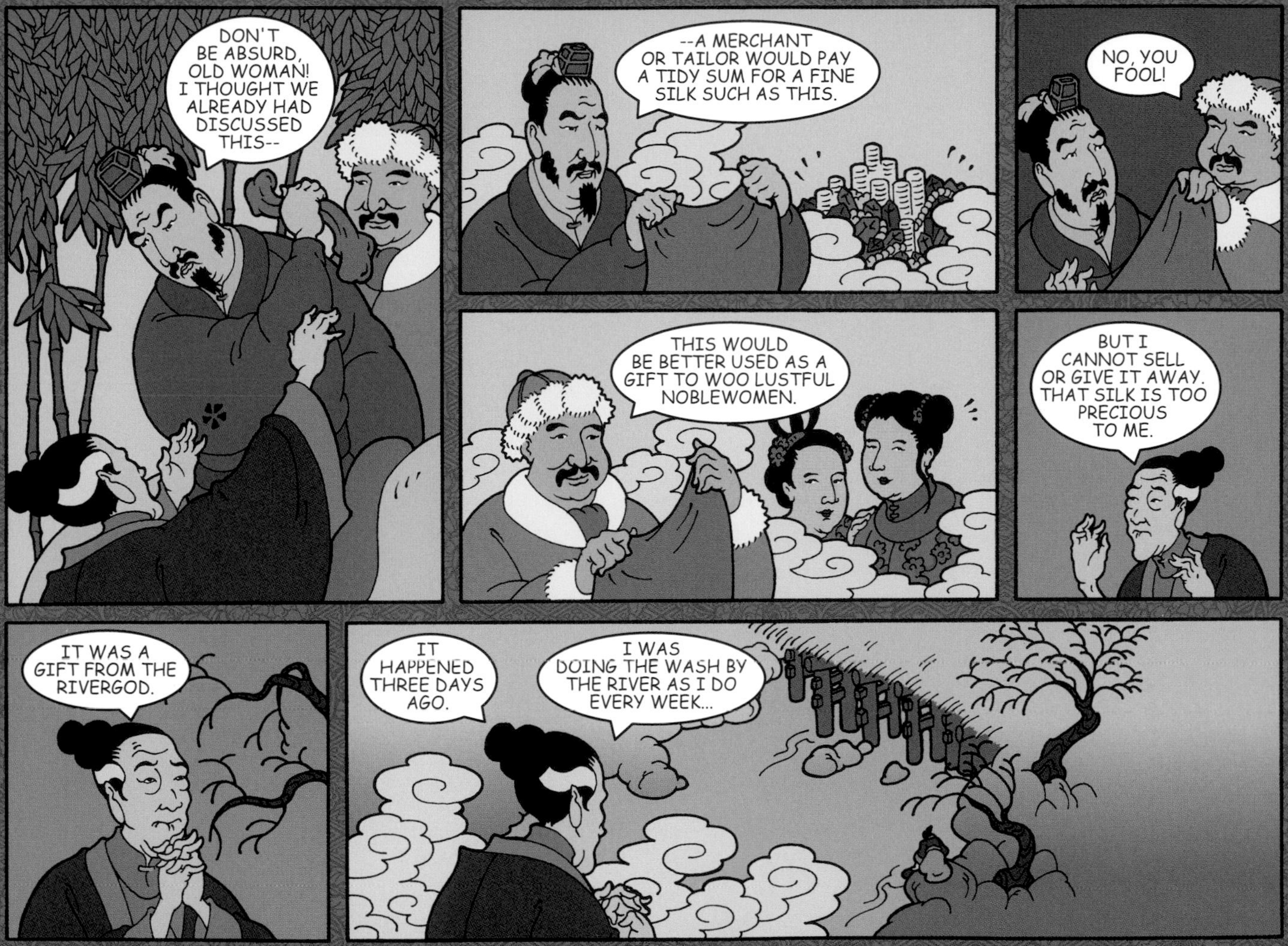
DON'T BE ABSURD, OLD WOMAN! I THOUGHT WE ALREADY HAD DISCUSSED THIS--
--A MERCHANT OR TAILOR WOULD PAY A TIDY SUM FOR A FINE SILK SUCH AS THIS.
NO, YOU FOOL!
THIS WOULD BE BETTER USED AS A GIFT TO WOO LUSTFUL NOBLEWOMEN.
BUT I CANNOT SELL OR GIVE IT AWAY. THAT SILK IS TOO PRECIOUS TO ME.
IT WAS A GIFT FROM THE RIVERGOD.
IT HAPPENED THREE DAYS AGO.
I WAS DOING THE WASH BY THE RIVER AS I DO EVERY WEEK...

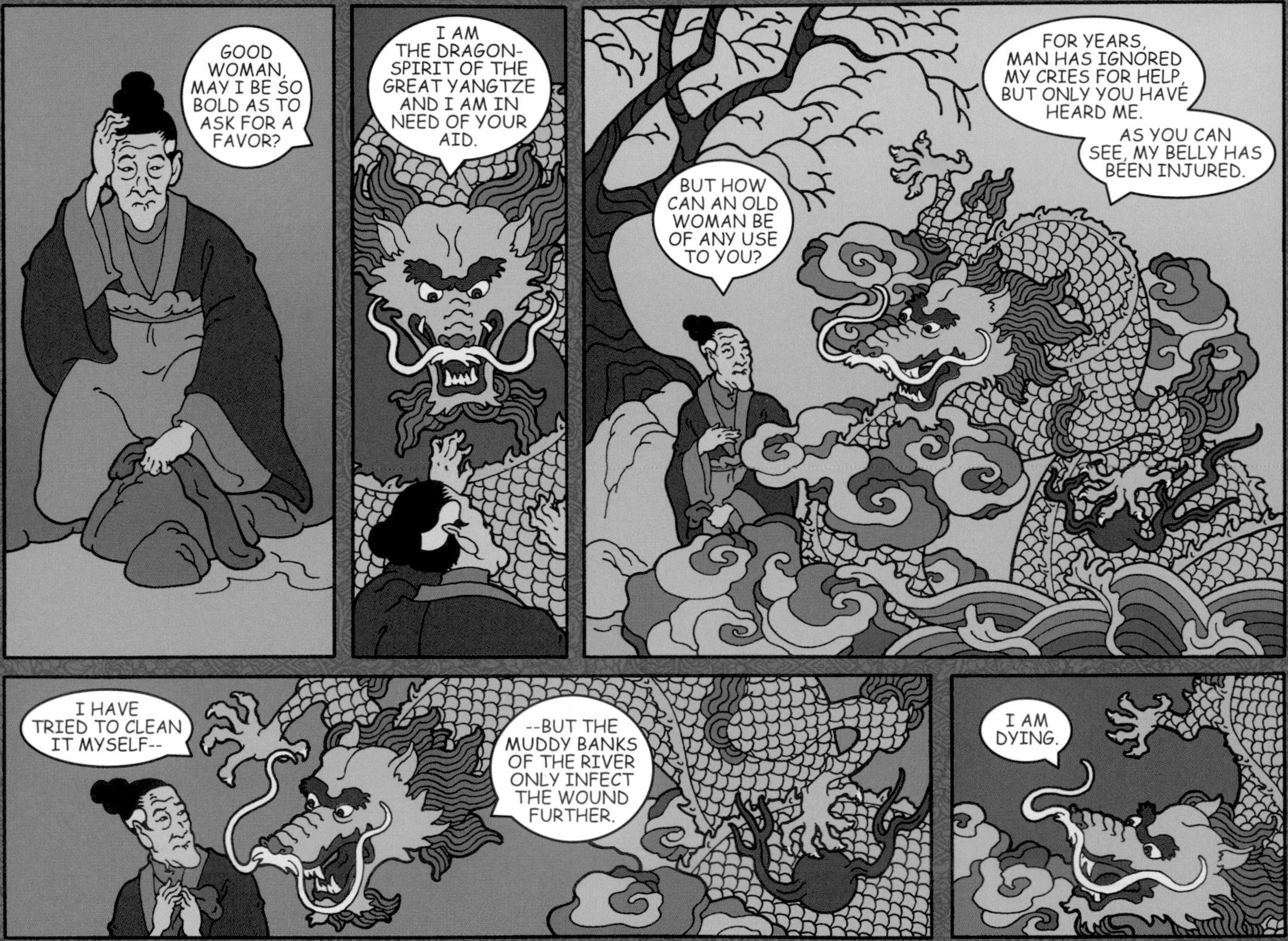
GOOD WOMAN, MAY I BE SO BOLD AS TO ASK FOR A FAVOR?
I AM THE DRAGON-SPIRIT OF THE GREAT YANGTZE AND I AM IN NEED OF YOUR AID.
BUT HOW CAN AN OLD WOMAN BE OF ANY USE TO YOU?
FOR YEARS, MAN HAS IGNORED MY CRIES FOR HELP, BUT ONLY YOU HAVE HEARD ME.
AS YOU CAN SEE, MY BELLY HAS BEEN INJURED.
I HAVE TRIED TO CLEAN IT MYSELF--
--BUT THE MUDDY BANKS OF THE RIVER ONLY INFECT THE WOUND FURTHER.
I AM DYING.

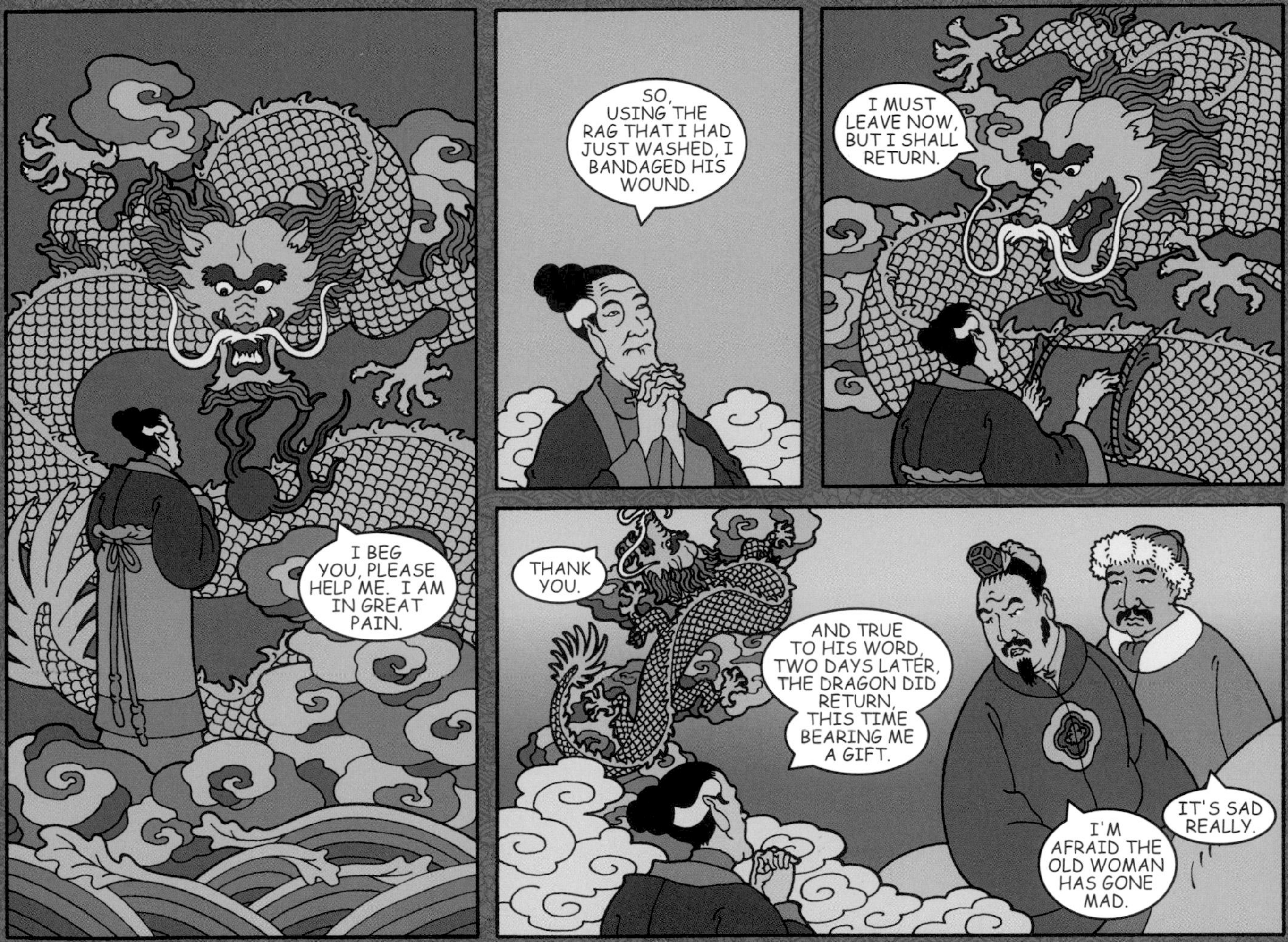
I BEG YOU, PLEASE HELP ME. I AM IN GREAT PAIN.
SO, USING THE RAG THAT I HAD JUST WASHED, I BANDAGED HIS WOUND.
I MUST LEAVE NOW, BUT I SHALL RETURN.
THANK YOU.
AND TRUE TO HIS WORD, TWO DAYS LATER, THE DRAGON DID RETURN, THIS TIME BEARING ME A GIFT.
I'M AFRAID THE OLD WOMAN HAS GONE MAD.
IT'S SAD REALLY.

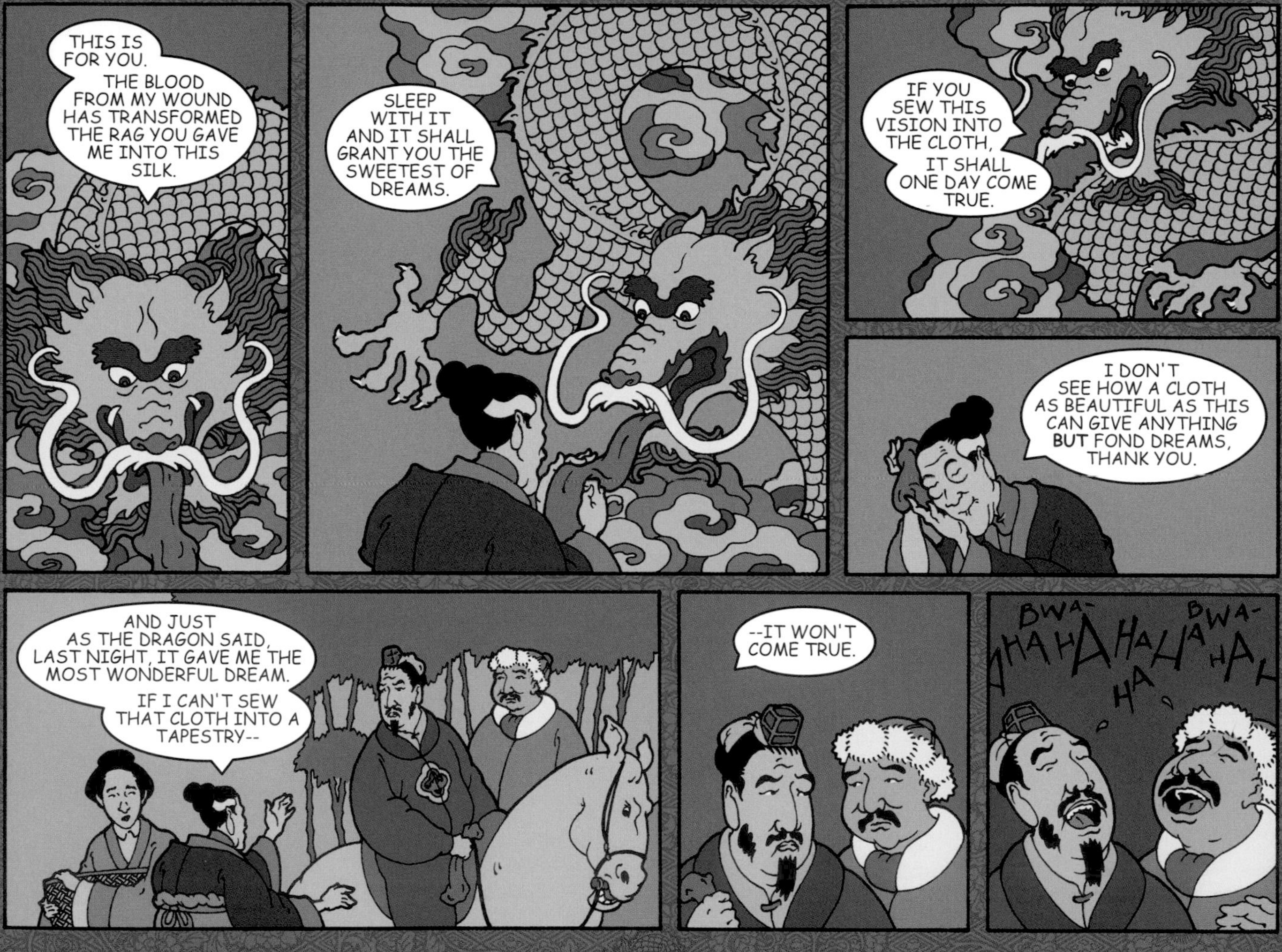
THIS IS FOR YOU.
THE BLOOD FROM MY WOUND HAS TRANSFORMED THE RAG YOU GAVE ME INTO THIS SILK.
SLEEP WITH IT AND IT SHALL GRANT YOU THE SWEETEST OF DREAMS.
IF YOU SEW THIS VISION INTO THE CLOTH,
IT SHALL ONE DAY COME TRUE.
I DON'T SEE HOW A CLOTH AS BEAUTIFUL AS THIS CAN GIVE ANYTHING **BUT** FOND DREAMS, THANK YOU.
AND JUST AS THE DRAGON SAID, LAST NIGHT, IT GAVE ME THE MOST WONDERFUL DREAM.
IF I CAN'T SEW THAT CLOTH INTO A TAPESTRY--
--IT WON'T COME TRUE.
BWA- BWA-
HAHAHAHAHAHA HAHAHA

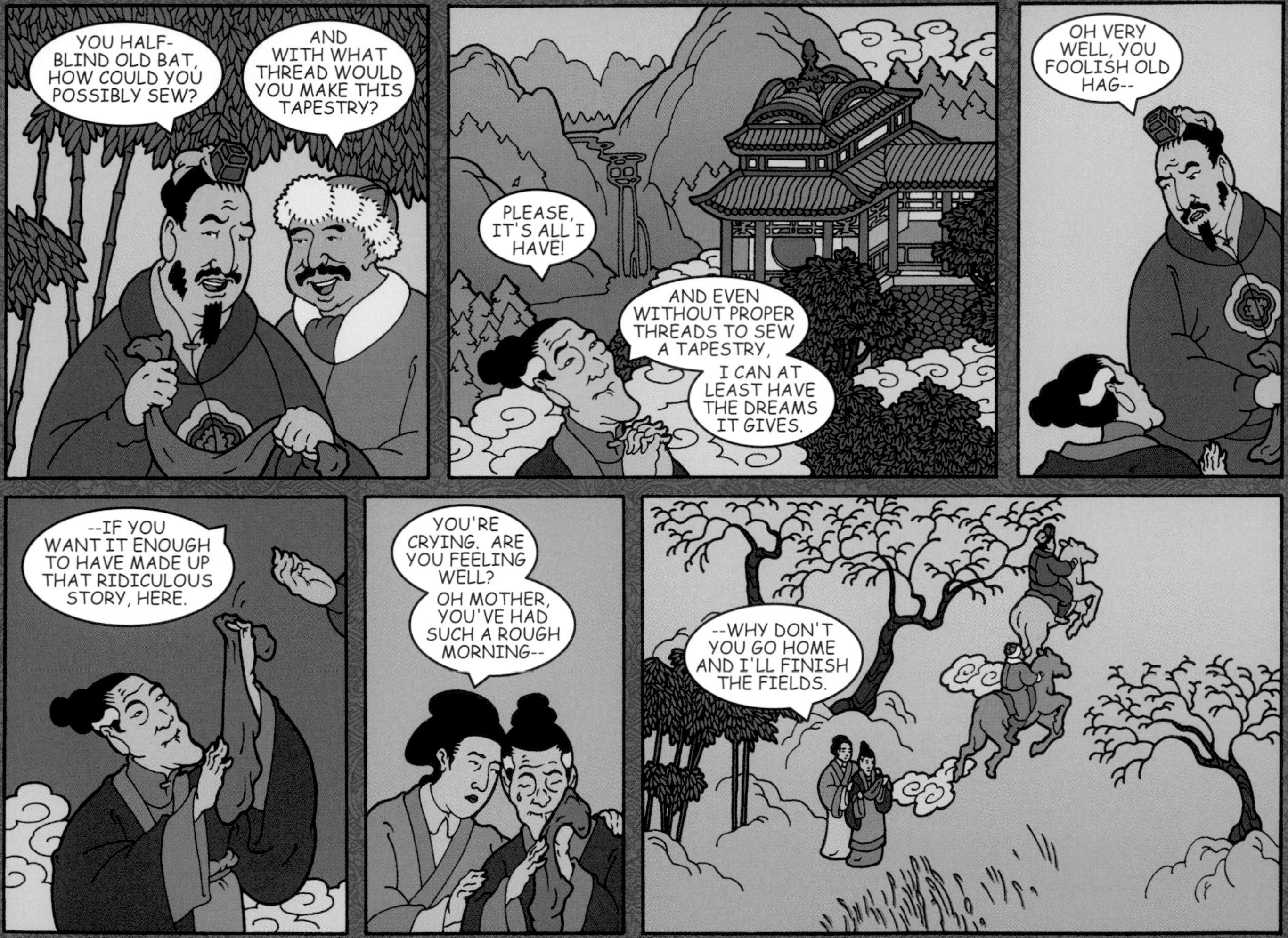
YOU HALF-BLIND OLD BAT, HOW COULD YOU POSSIBLY SEW?
AND WITH WHAT THREAD WOULD YOU MAKE THIS TAPESTRY?
PLEASE, IT'S ALL I HAVE!
AND EVEN WITHOUT PROPER THREADS TO SEW A TAPESTRY,
I CAN AT LEAST HAVE THE DREAMS IT GIVES.
OH VERY WELL, YOU FOOLISH OLD HAG--
--IF YOU WANT IT ENOUGH TO HAVE MADE UP THAT RIDICULOUS STORY, HERE.
YOU'RE CRYING. ARE YOU FEELING WELL?
OH MOTHER, YOU'VE HAD SUCH A ROUGH MORNING--
--WHY DON'T YOU GO HOME AND I'LL FINISH THE FIELDS.

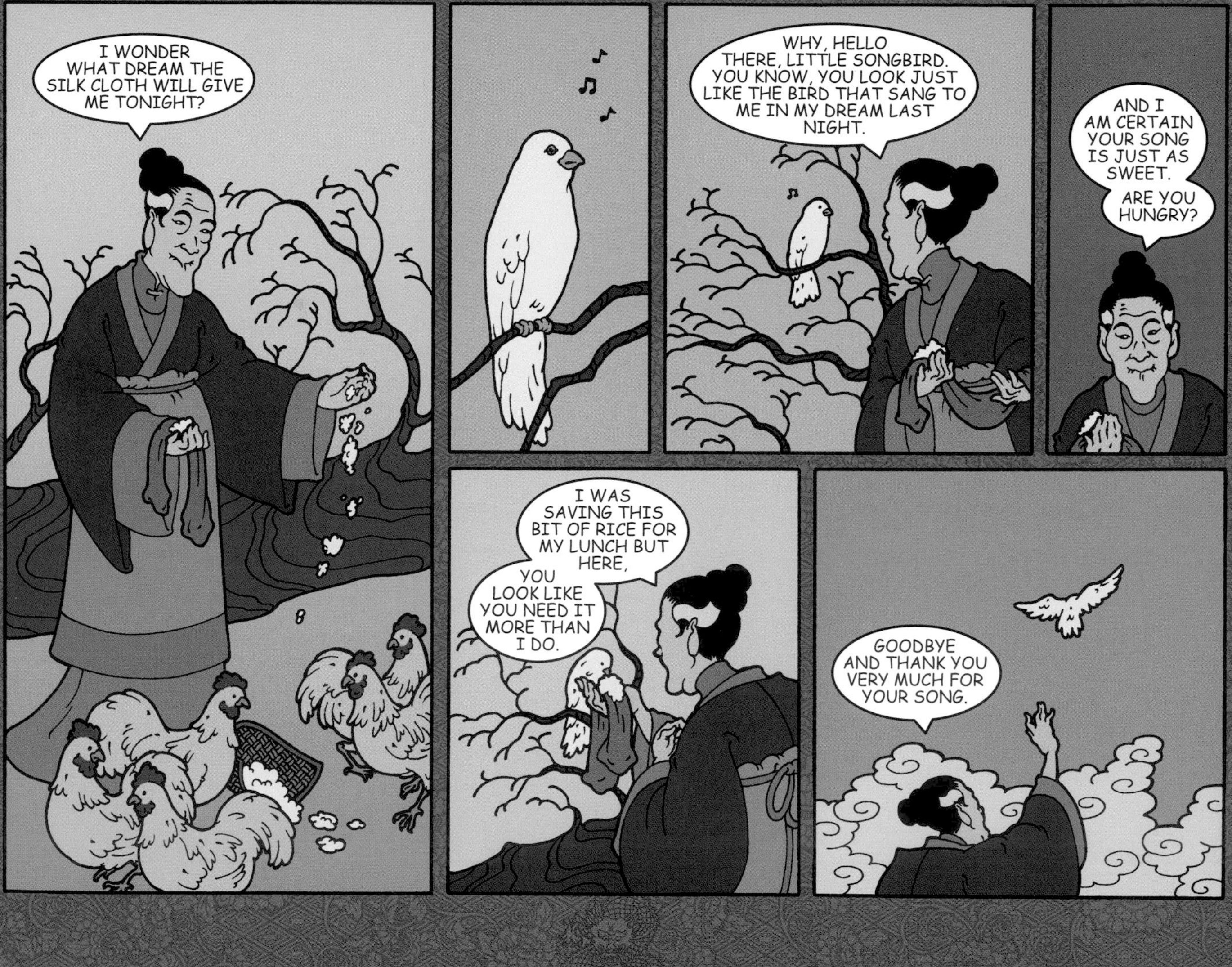
I WONDER WHAT DREAM THE SILK CLOTH WILL GIVE ME TONIGHT?
WHY, HELLO THERE, LITTLE SONGBIRD. YOU KNOW, YOU LOOK JUST LIKE THE BIRD THAT SANG TO ME IN MY DREAM LAST NIGHT.
AND I AM CERTAIN YOUR SONG IS JUST AS SWEET.
ARE YOU HUNGRY?
I WAS SAVING THIS BIT OF RICE FOR MY LUNCH BUT HERE,
YOU LOOK LIKE YOU NEED IT MORE THAN I DO.
GOODBYE AND THANK YOU VERY MUCH FOR YOUR SONG.

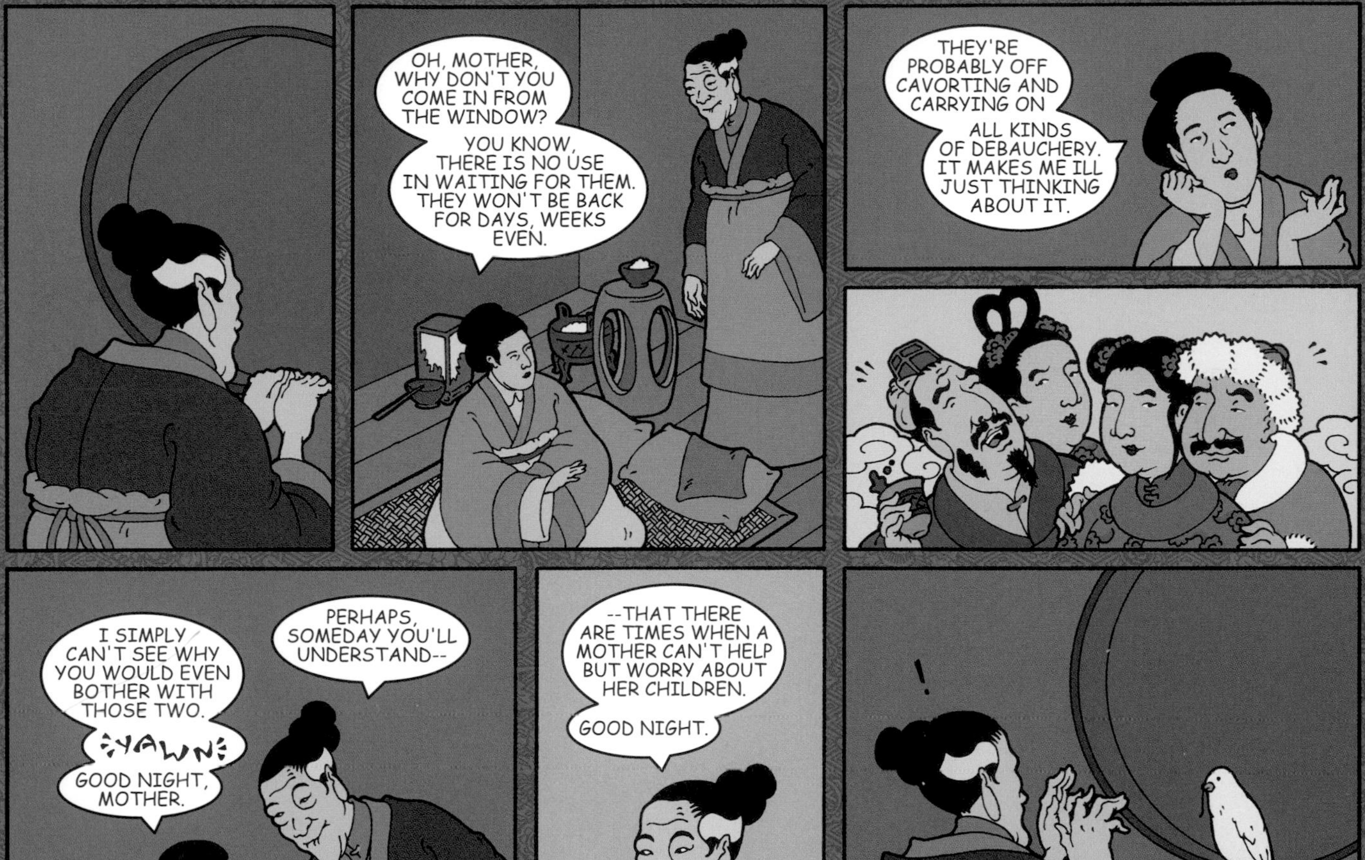
OH, MOTHER, WHY DON'T YOU COME IN FROM THE WINDOW?
YOU KNOW, THERE IS NO USE IN WAITING FOR THEM. THEY WON'T BE BACK FOR DAYS, WEEKS EVEN.
THEY'RE PROBABLY OFF CAVORTING AND CARRYING ON
ALL KINDS OF DEBAUCHERY. IT MAKES ME ILL JUST THINKING ABOUT IT.
I SIMPLY CAN'T SEE WHY YOU WOULD EVEN BOTHER WITH THOSE TWO.
YAWN
GOOD NIGHT, MOTHER.
PERHAPS, SOMEDAY YOU'LL UNDERSTAND--
--THAT THERE ARE TIMES WHEN A MOTHER CAN'T HELP BUT WORRY ABOUT HER CHILDREN.
GOOD NIGHT.
!

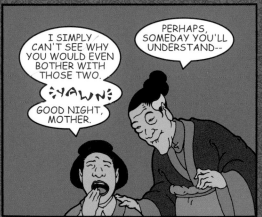

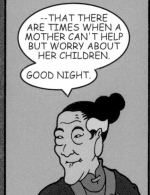

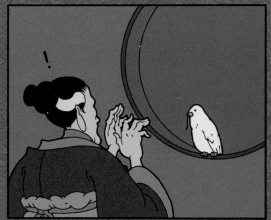

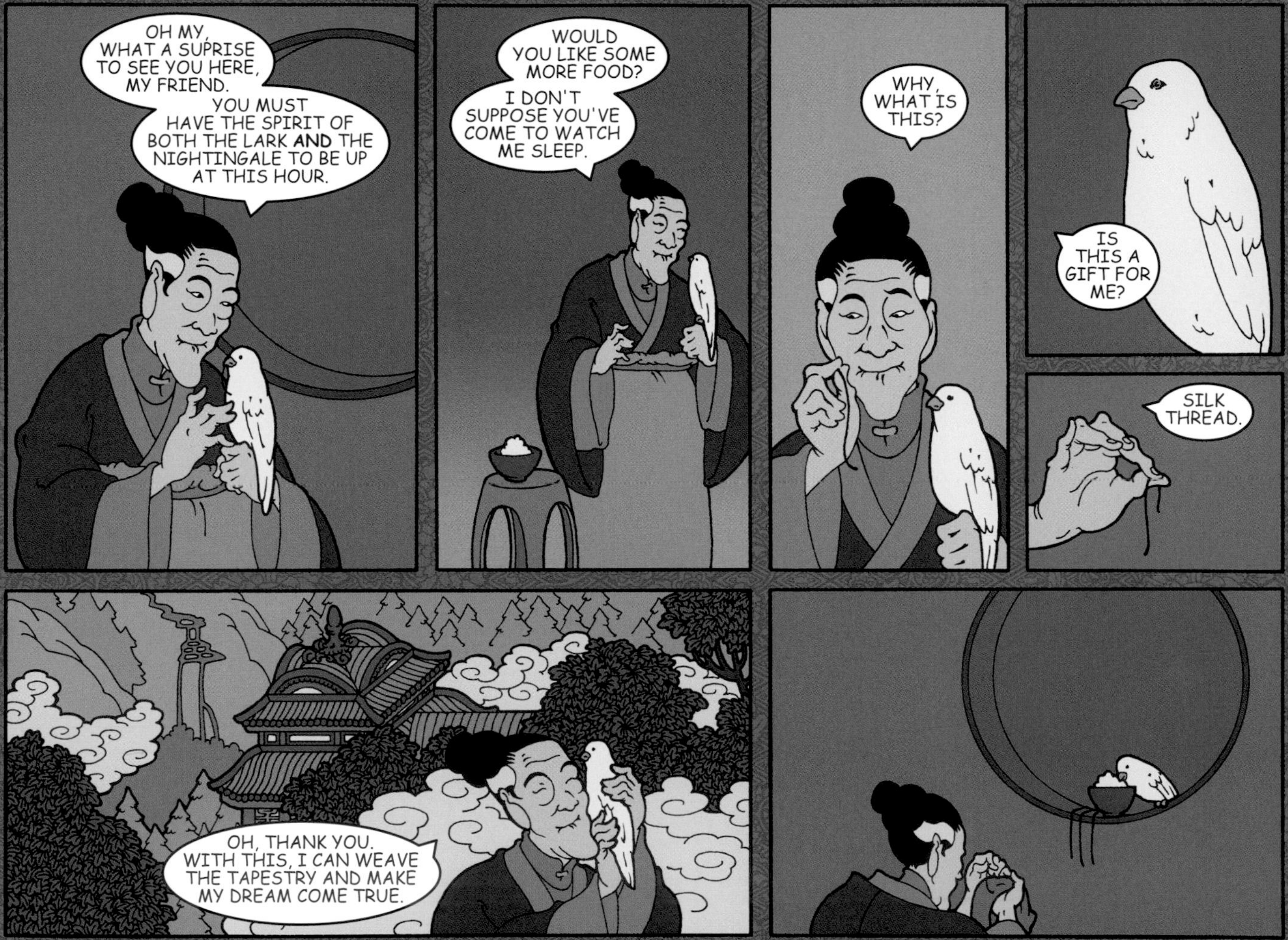
OH MY, WHAT A SUPRISE TO SEE YOU HERE, MY FRIEND.
YOU MUST HAVE THE SPIRIT OF BOTH THE LARK **AND** THE NIGHTINGALE TO BE UP AT THIS HOUR.
WOULD YOU LIKE SOME MORE FOOD?
I DON'T SUPPOSE YOU'VE COME TO WATCH ME SLEEP.
WHY, WHAT IS THIS?
IS THIS A GIFT FOR ME?
SILK THREAD.
OH, THANK YOU. WITH THIS, I CAN WEAVE THE TAPESTRY AND MAKE MY DREAM COME TRUE.

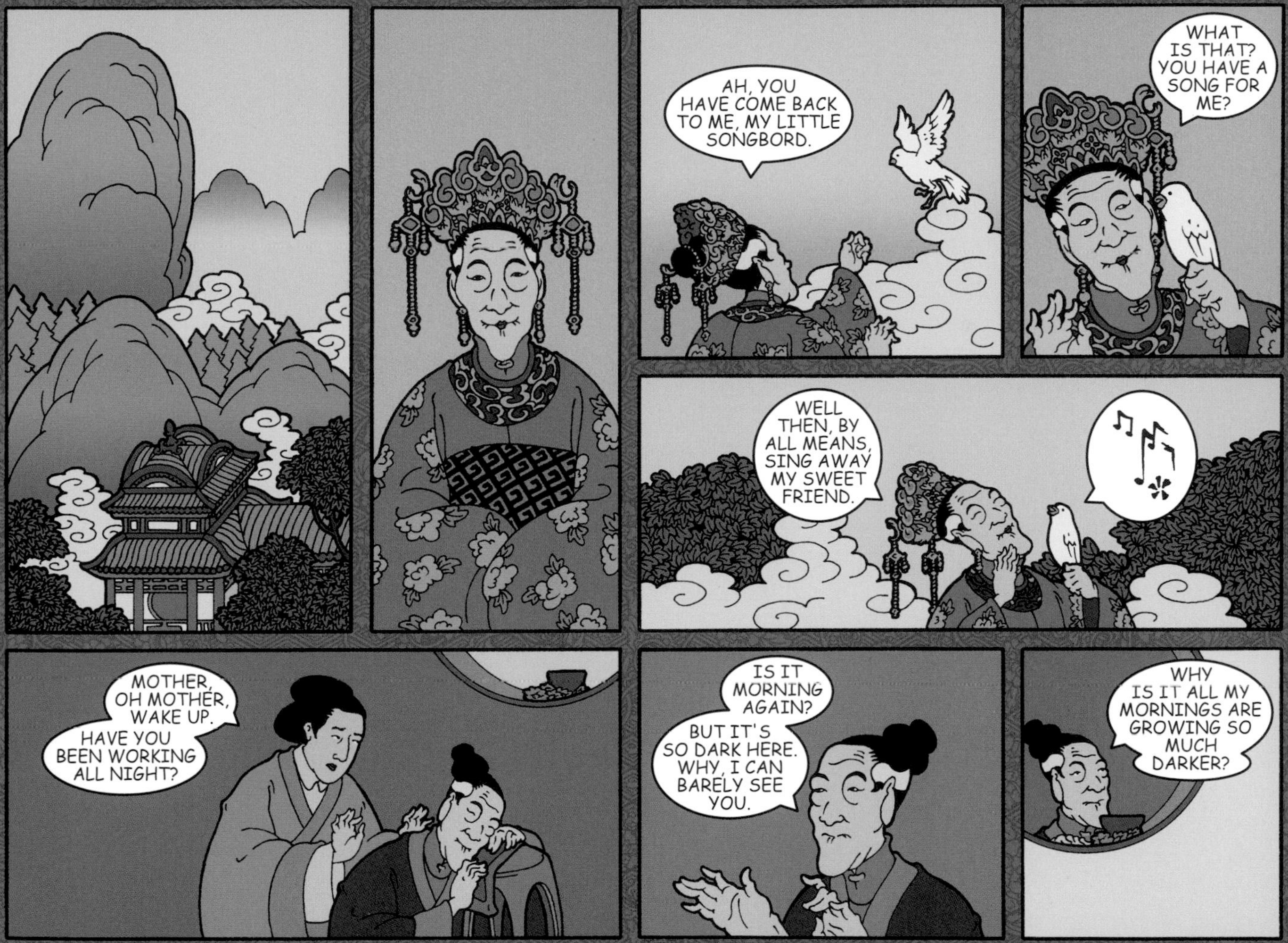
AH, YOU HAVE COME BACK TO ME, MY LITTLE SONGBORD.
WHAT IS THAT? YOU HAVE A SONG FOR ME?
WELL THEN, BY ALL MEANS, SING AWAY MY SWEET FRIEND.
MOTHER, OH MOTHER, WAKE UP.
HAVE YOU BEEN WORKING ALL NIGHT?
IS IT MORNING AGAIN?
BUT IT'S SO DARK HERE. WHY, I CAN BARELY SEE YOU.
WHY IS IT ALL MY MORNINGS ARE GROWING SO MUCH DARKER?

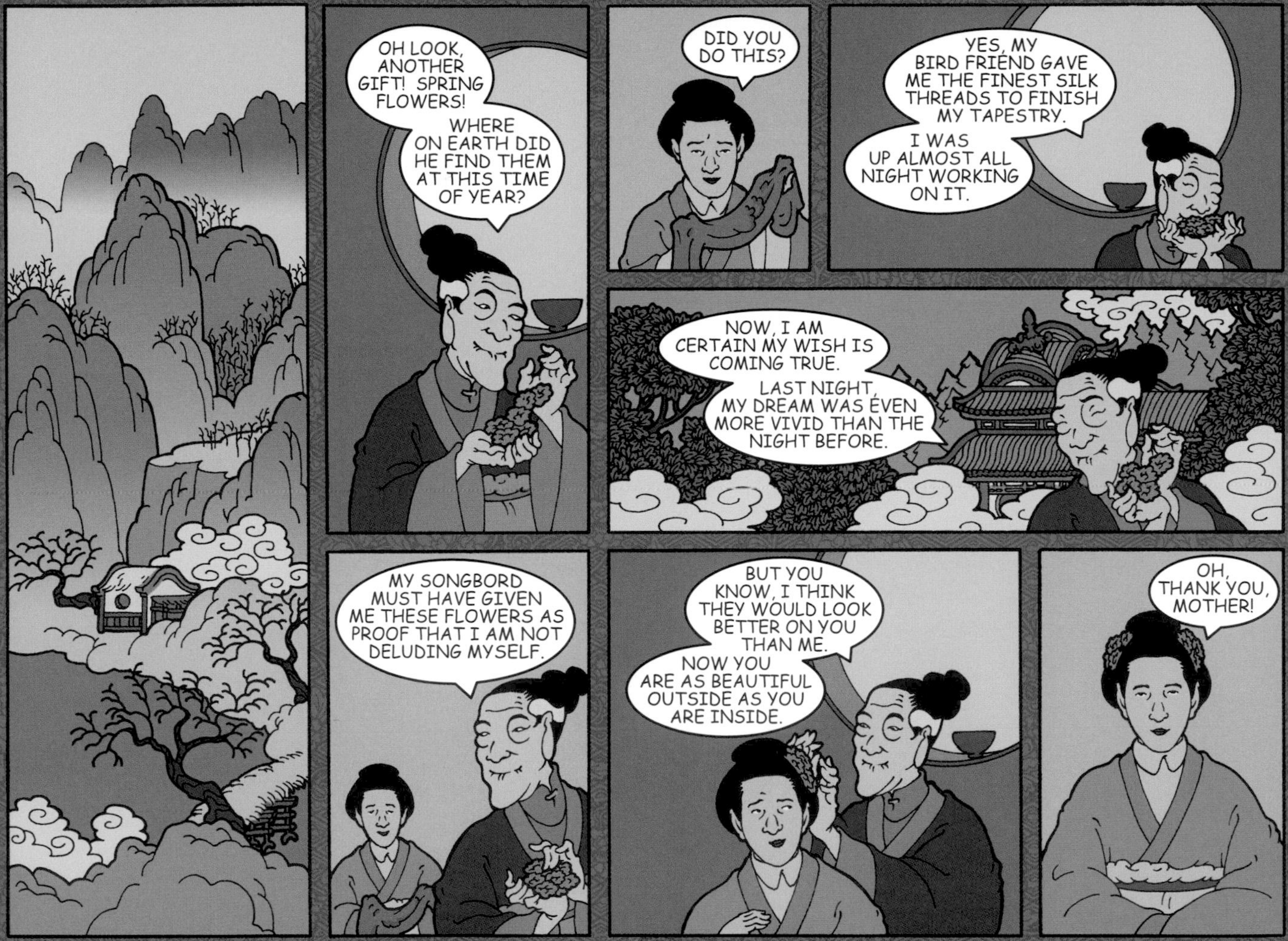
OH LOOK, ANOTHER GIFT! SPRING FLOWERS!
WHERE ON EARTH DID HE FIND THEM AT THIS TIME OF YEAR?
DID YOU DO THIS?
YES, MY BIRD FRIEND GAVE ME THE FINEST SILK THREADS TO FINISH MY TAPESTRY.
I WAS UP ALMOST ALL NIGHT WORKING ON IT.
NOW, I AM CERTAIN MY WISH IS COMING TRUE.
LAST NIGHT, MY DREAM WAS EVEN MORE VIVID THAN THE NIGHT BEFORE.
MY SONGBORD MUST HAVE GIVEN ME THESE FLOWERS AS PROOF THAT I AM NOT DELUDING MYSELF.
BUT YOU KNOW, I THINK THEY WOULD LOOK BETTER ON YOU THAN ME.
NOW YOU ARE AS BEAUTIFUL OUTSIDE AS YOU ARE INSIDE.
OH, THANK YOU, MOTHER!

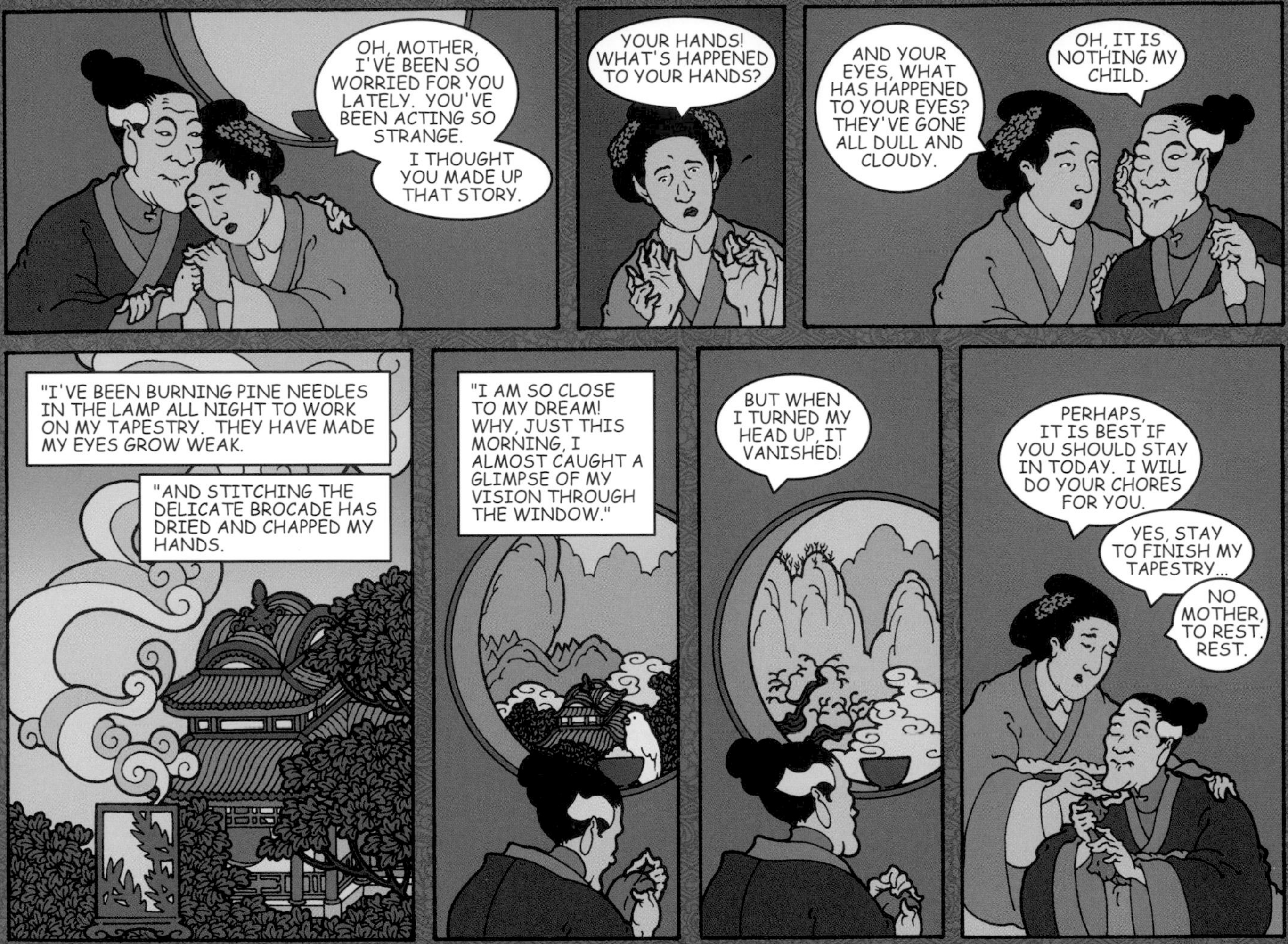
OH, MOTHER, I'VE BEEN SO WORRIED FOR YOU LATELY. YOU'VE BEEN ACTING SO STRANGE.
I THOUGHT YOU MADE UP THAT STORY.
YOUR HANDS! WHAT'S HAPPENED TO YOUR HANDS?
AND YOUR EYES, WHAT HAS HAPPENED TO YOUR EYES? THEY'VE GONE ALL DULL AND CLOUDY.
OH, IT IS NOTHING MY CHILD.
"I'VE BEEN BURNING PINE NEEDLES IN THE LAMP ALL NIGHT TO WORK ON MY TAPESTRY. THEY HAVE MADE MY EYES GROW WEAK.
"AND STITCHING THE DELICATE BROCADE HAS DRIED AND CHAPPED MY HANDS.
"I AM SO CLOSE TO MY DREAM! WHY, JUST THIS MORNING, I ALMOST CAUGHT A GLIMPSE OF MY VISION THROUGH THE WINDOW."
BUT WHEN I TURNED MY HEAD UP, IT VANISHED!
PERHAPS, IT IS BEST IF YOU SHOULD STAY IN TODAY. I WILL DO YOUR CHORES FOR YOU.
YES, STAY TO FINISH MY TAPESTRY...
NO MOTHER, TO REST. REST.

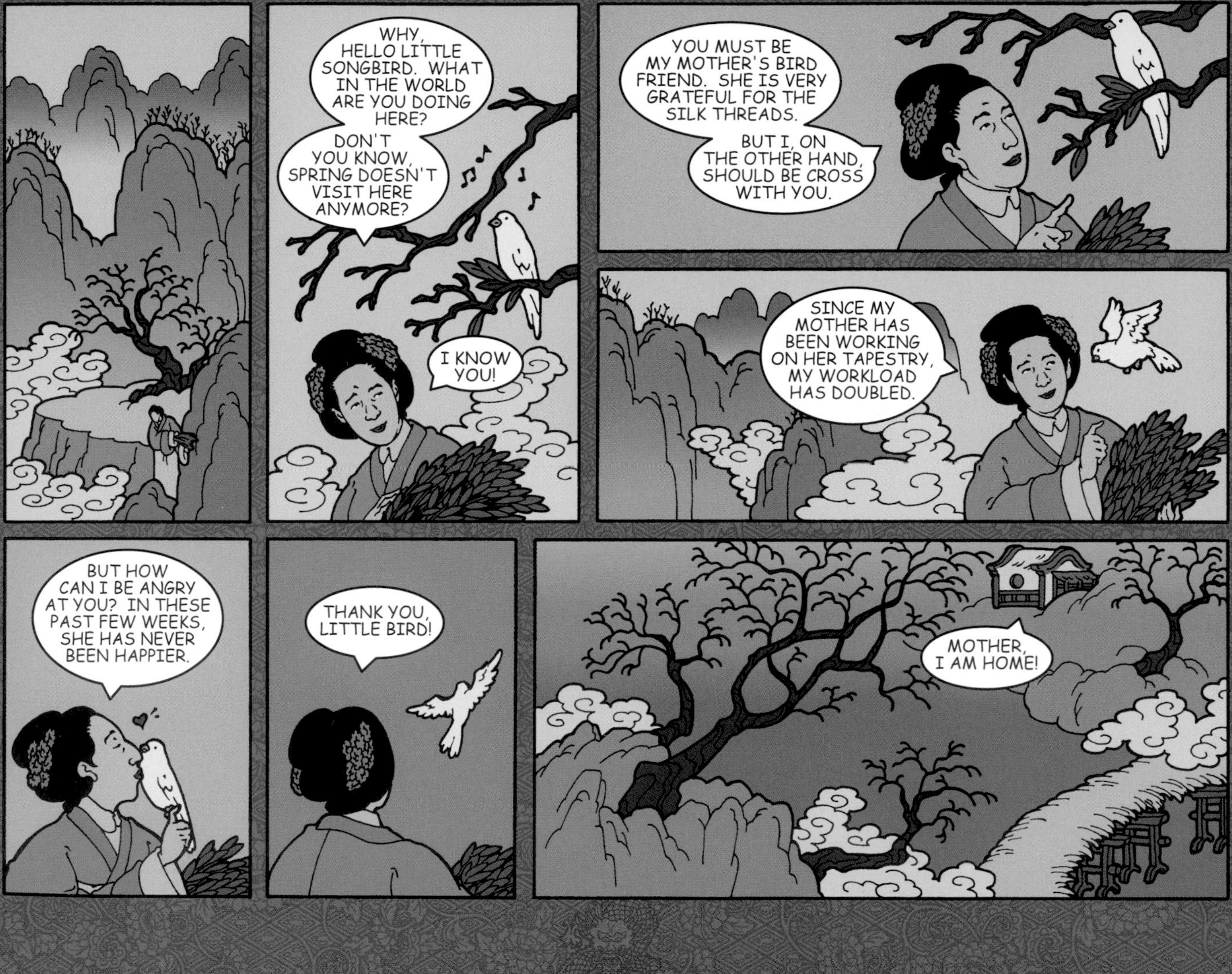
WHY, HELLO LITTLE SONGBIRD. WHAT IN THE WORLD ARE YOU DOING HERE?
DON'T YOU KNOW, SPRING DOESN'T VISIT HERE ANYMORE?
I KNOW YOU!
YOU MUST BE MY MOTHER'S BIRD FRIEND. SHE IS VERY GRATEFUL FOR THE SILK THREADS.
BUT I, ON THE OTHER HAND, SHOULD BE CROSS WITH YOU.
SINCE MY MOTHER HAS BEEN WORKING ON HER TAPESTRY, MY WORKLOAD HAS DOUBLED.
BUT HOW CAN I BE ANGRY AT YOU? IN THESE PAST FEW WEEKS, SHE HAS NEVER BEEN HAPPIER.
THANK YOU, LITTLE BIRD!
MOTHER, I AM HOME!

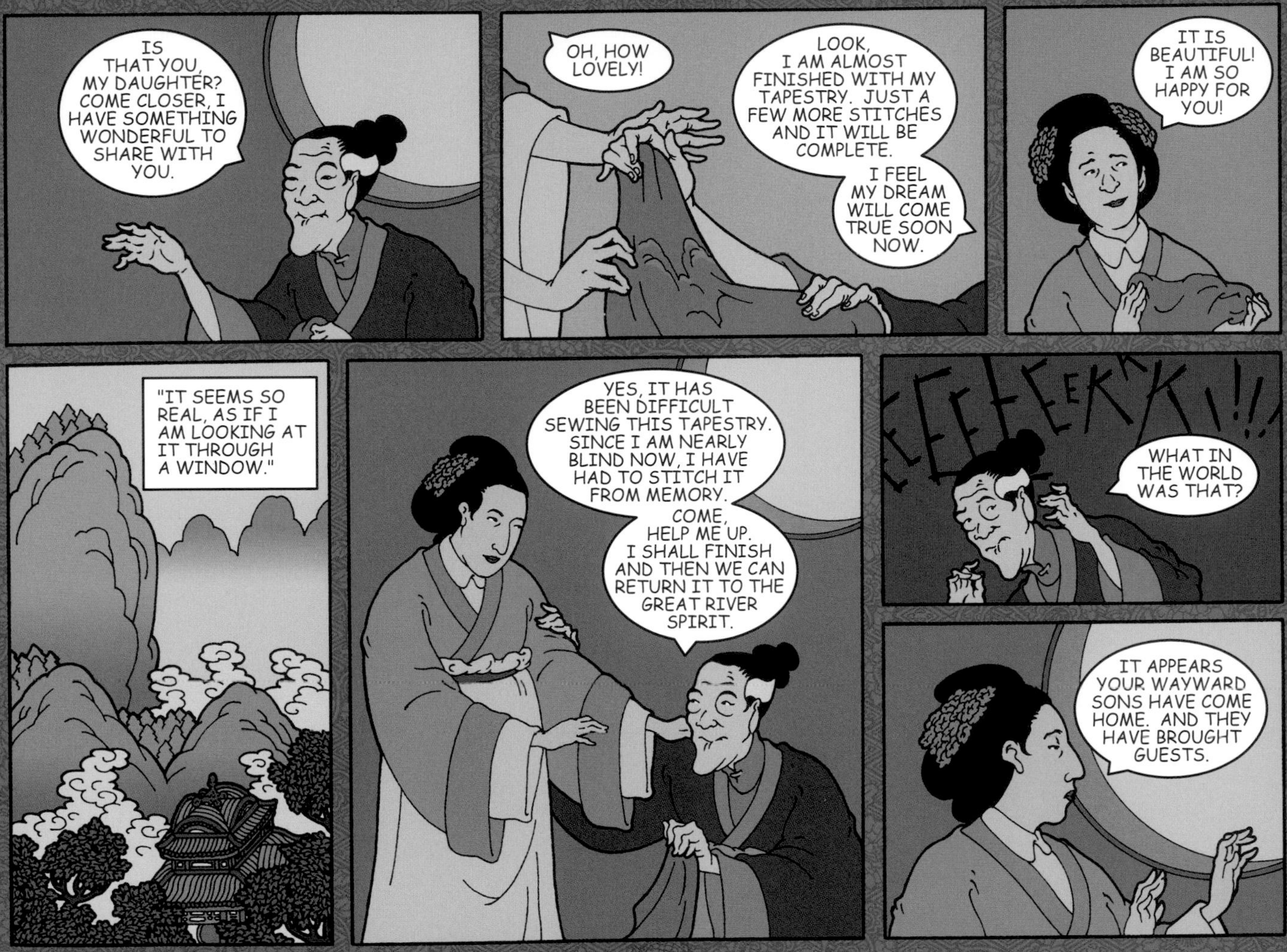
IS THAT YOU, MY DAUGHTER? COME CLOSER, I HAVE SOMETHING WONDERFUL TO SHARE WITH YOU.
OH, HOW LOVELY!
LOOK, I AM ALMOST FINISHED WITH MY TAPESTRY. JUST A FEW MORE STITCHES AND IT WILL BE COMPLETE.
I FEEL MY DREAM WILL COME TRUE SOON NOW.
IT IS BEAUTIFUL! I AM SO HAPPY FOR YOU!
"IT SEEMS SO REAL, AS IF I AM LOOKING AT IT THROUGH A WINDOW."
YES, IT HAS BEEN DIFFICULT SEWING THIS TAPESTRY. SINCE I AM NEARLY BLIND NOW, I HAVE HAD TO STITCH IT FROM MEMORY.
COME, HELP ME UP. I SHALL FINISH AND THEN WE CAN RETURN IT TO THE GREAT RIVER SPIRIT.
EEEEEKKK!!!
WHAT IN THE WORLD WAS THAT?
IT APPEARS YOUR WAYWARD SONS HAVE COME HOME. AND THEY HAVE BROUGHT GUESTS.

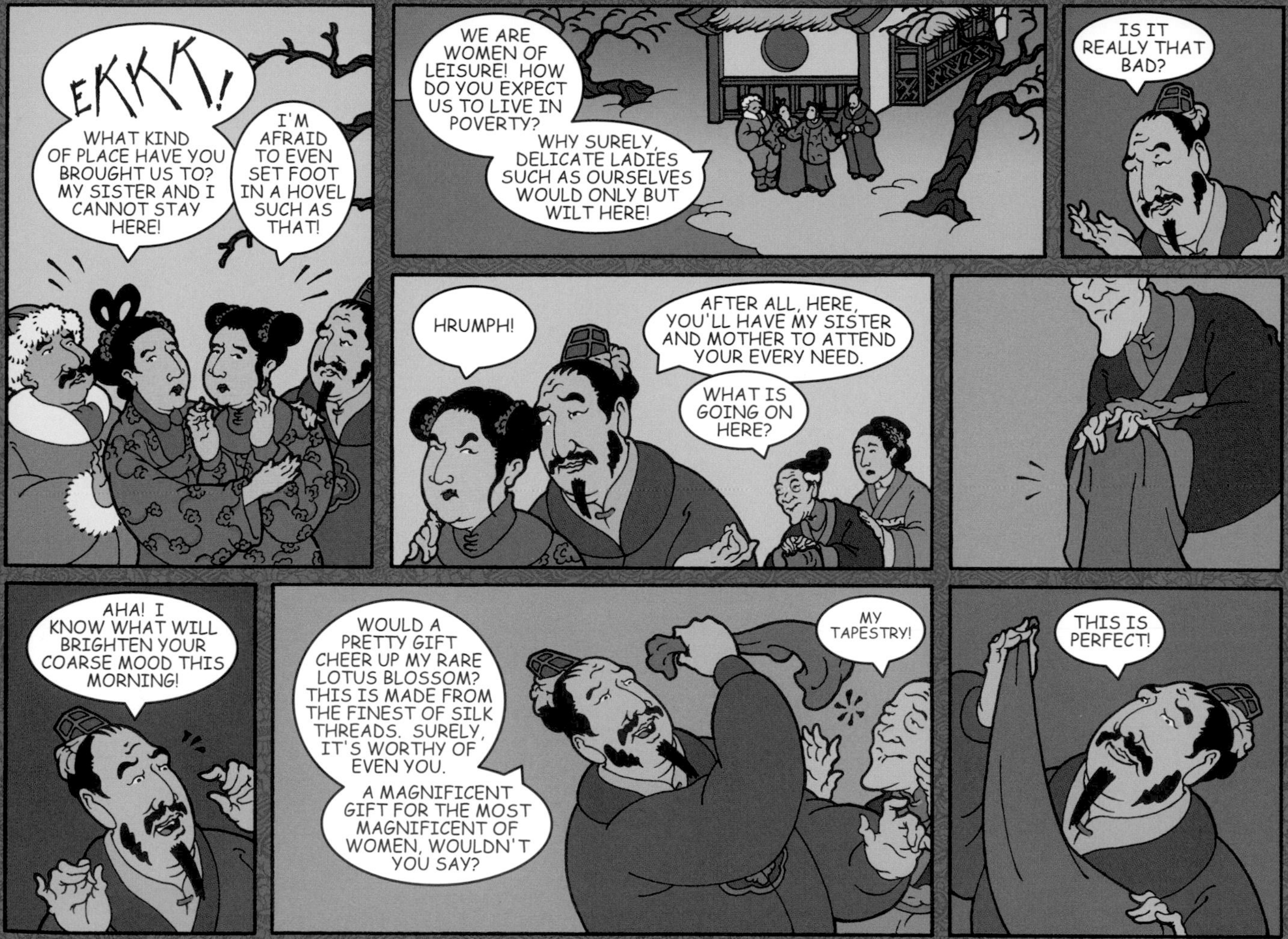
EKKK!
WHAT KIND OF PLACE HAVE YOU BROUGHT US TO? MY SISTER AND I CANNOT STAY HERE!
I'M AFRAID TO EVEN SET FOOT IN A HOVEL SUCH AS THAT!
WE ARE WOMEN OF LEISURE! HOW DO YOU EXPECT US TO LIVE IN POVERTY?
WHY SURELY, DELICATE LADIES SUCH AS OURSELVES WOULD ONLY BUT WILT HERE!
IS IT REALLY THAT BAD?
HRUMPH!
AFTER ALL, HERE, YOU'LL HAVE MY SISTER AND MOTHER TO ATTEND YOUR EVERY NEED.
WHAT IS GOING ON HERE?
AHA! I KNOW WHAT WILL BRIGHTEN YOUR COARSE MOOD THIS MORNING!
WOULD A PRETTY GIFT CHEER UP MY RARE LOTUS BLOSSOM? THIS IS MADE FROM THE FINEST OF SILK THREADS. SURELY, IT'S WORTHY OF EVEN YOU.
A MAGNIFICENT GIFT FOR THE MOST MAGNIFICENT OF WOMEN, WOULDN'T YOU SAY?
MY TAPESTRY!
THIS IS PERFECT!

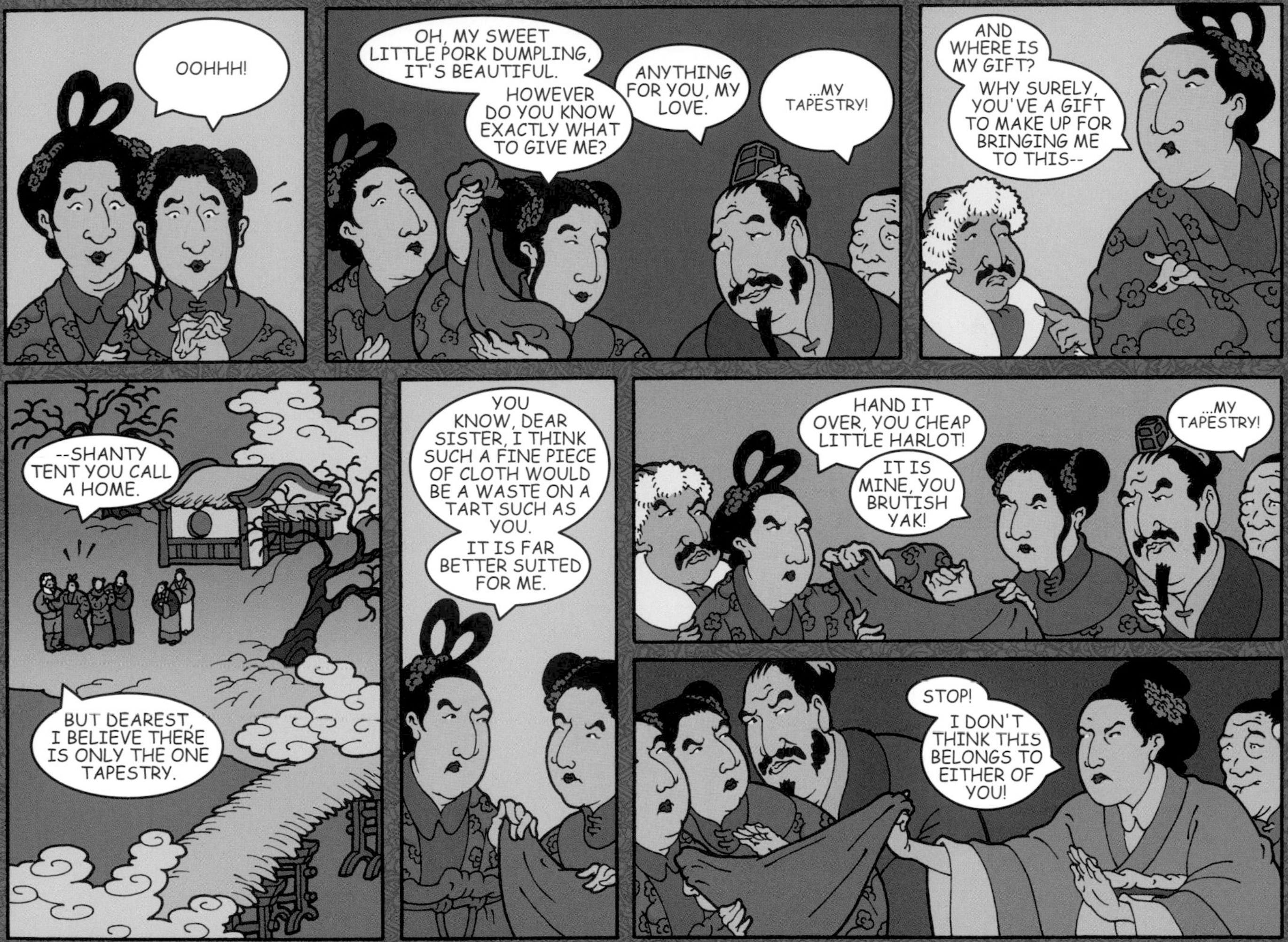
OOHHH!
OH, MY SWEET LITTLE PORK DUMPLING, IT'S BEAUTIFUL.
HOWEVER DO YOU KNOW EXACTLY WHAT TO GIVE ME?
ANYTHING FOR YOU, MY LOVE.
...MY TAPESTRY!
AND WHERE IS MY GIFT?
WHY SURELY, YOU'VE A GIFT TO MAKE UP FOR BRINGING ME TO THIS--
--SHANTY TENT YOU CALL A HOME.
BUT DEAREST, I BELIEVE THERE IS ONLY THE ONE TAPESTRY.
YOU KNOW, DEAR SISTER, I THINK SUCH A FINE PIECE OF CLOTH WOULD BE A WASTE ON A TART SUCH AS YOU.
IT IS FAR BETTER SUITED FOR ME.
HAND IT OVER, YOU CHEAP LITTLE HARLOT!
IT IS MINE, YOU BRUTISH YAK!
...MY TAPESTRY!
STOP!
I DON'T THINK THIS BELONGS TO EITHER OF YOU!

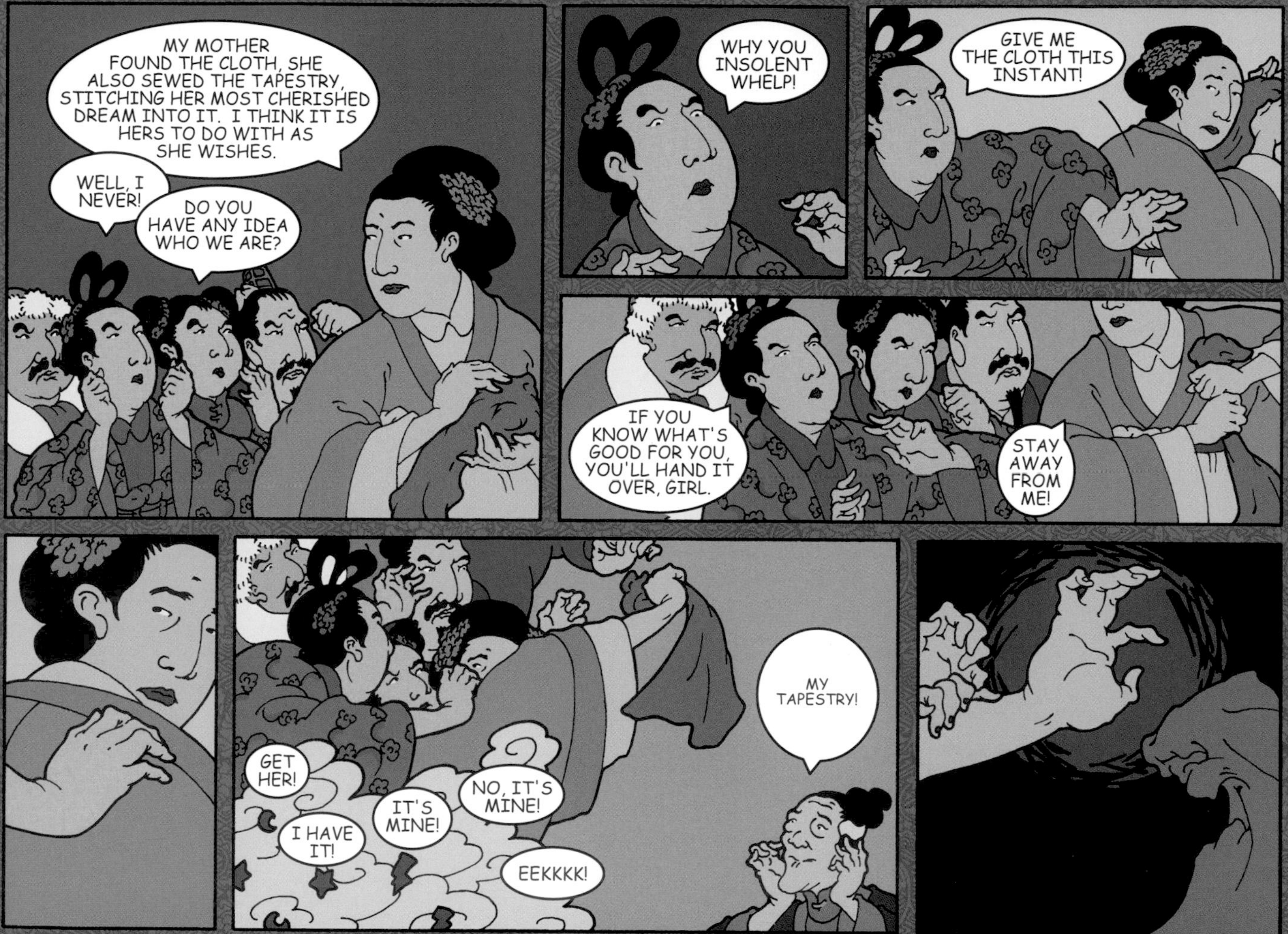
MY MOTHER FOUND THE CLOTH, SHE ALSO SEWED THE TAPESTRY, STITCHING HER MOST CHERISHED DREAM INTO IT. I THINK IT IS HERS TO DO WITH AS SHE WISHES.
WELL, I NEVER!
DO YOU HAVE ANY IDEA WHO WE ARE?
WHY YOU INSOLENT WHELP!
GIVE ME THE CLOTH THIS INSTANT!
IF YOU KNOW WHAT'S GOOD FOR YOU, YOU'LL HAND IT OVER, GIRL.
STAY AWAY FROM ME!
MY TAPESTRY!
GET HER!
I HAVE IT!
IT'S MINE!
NO, IT'S MINE!
EEKKKK!

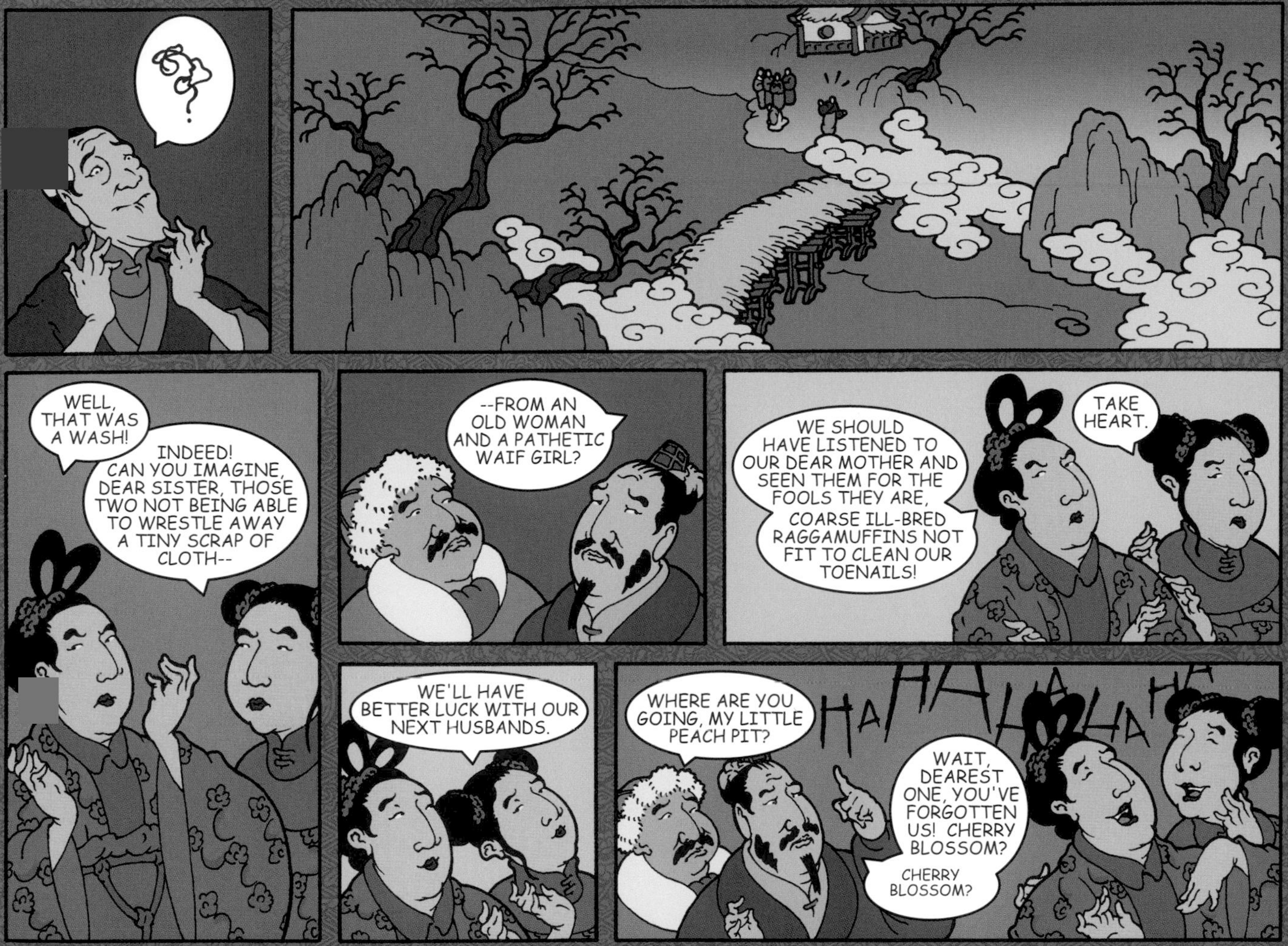
WELL, THAT WAS A WASH!
INDEED! CAN YOU IMAGINE, DEAR SISTER, THOSE TWO NOT BEING ABLE TO WRESTLE AWAY A TINY SCRAP OF CLOTH--
--FROM AN OLD WOMAN AND A PATHETIC WAIF GIRL?
WE SHOULD HAVE LISTENED TO OUR DEAR MOTHER AND SEEN THEM FOR THE FOOLS THEY ARE,
COARSE ILL-BRED RAGGAMUFFINS NOT FIT TO CLEAN OUR TOENAILS!
TAKE HEART.
WE'LL HAVE BETTER LUCK WITH OUR NEXT HUSBANDS.
WHERE ARE YOU GOING, MY LITTLE PEACH PIT?
HA HA HA HA HA HA
WAIT, DEAREST ONE, YOU'VE FORGOTTEN US! CHERRY BLOSSOM?
CHERRY BLOSSOM?

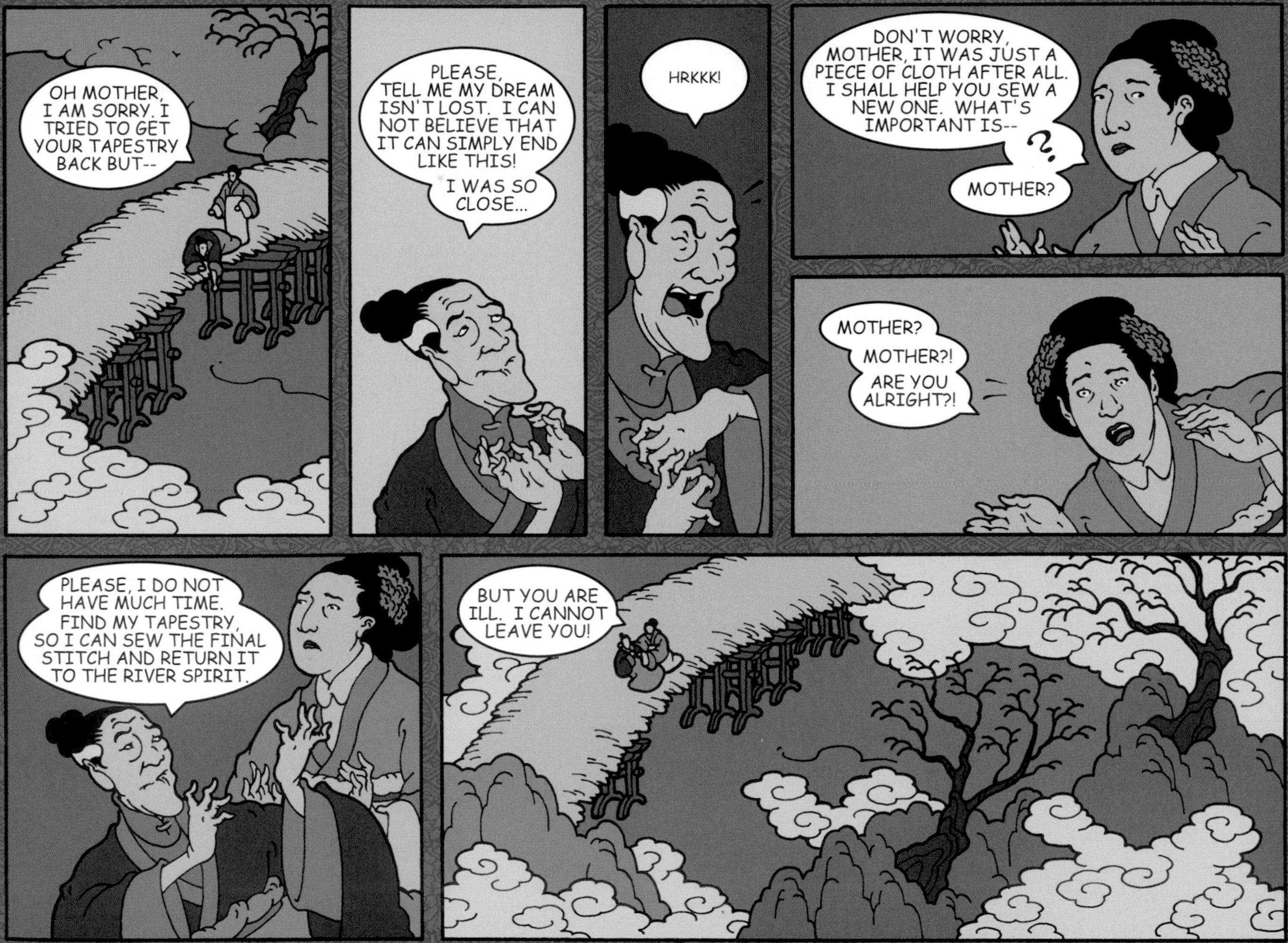
OH MOTHER, I AM SORRY. I TRIED TO GET YOUR TAPESTRY BACK BUT--
PLEASE, TELL ME MY DREAM ISN'T LOST. I CAN NOT BELIEVE THAT IT CAN SIMPLY END LIKE THIS!
I WAS SO CLOSE...
HRKKK!
DON'T WORRY, MOTHER, IT WAS JUST A PIECE OF CLOTH AFTER ALL. I SHALL HELP YOU SEW A NEW ONE. WHAT'S IMPORTANT IS--
?
MOTHER?
MOTHER?
MOTHER?!
ARE YOU ALRIGHT?!
PLEASE, I DO NOT HAVE MUCH TIME. FIND MY TAPESTRY, SO I CAN SEW THE FINAL STITCH AND RETURN IT TO THE RIVER SPIRIT.
BUT YOU ARE ILL. I CANNOT LEAVE YOU!

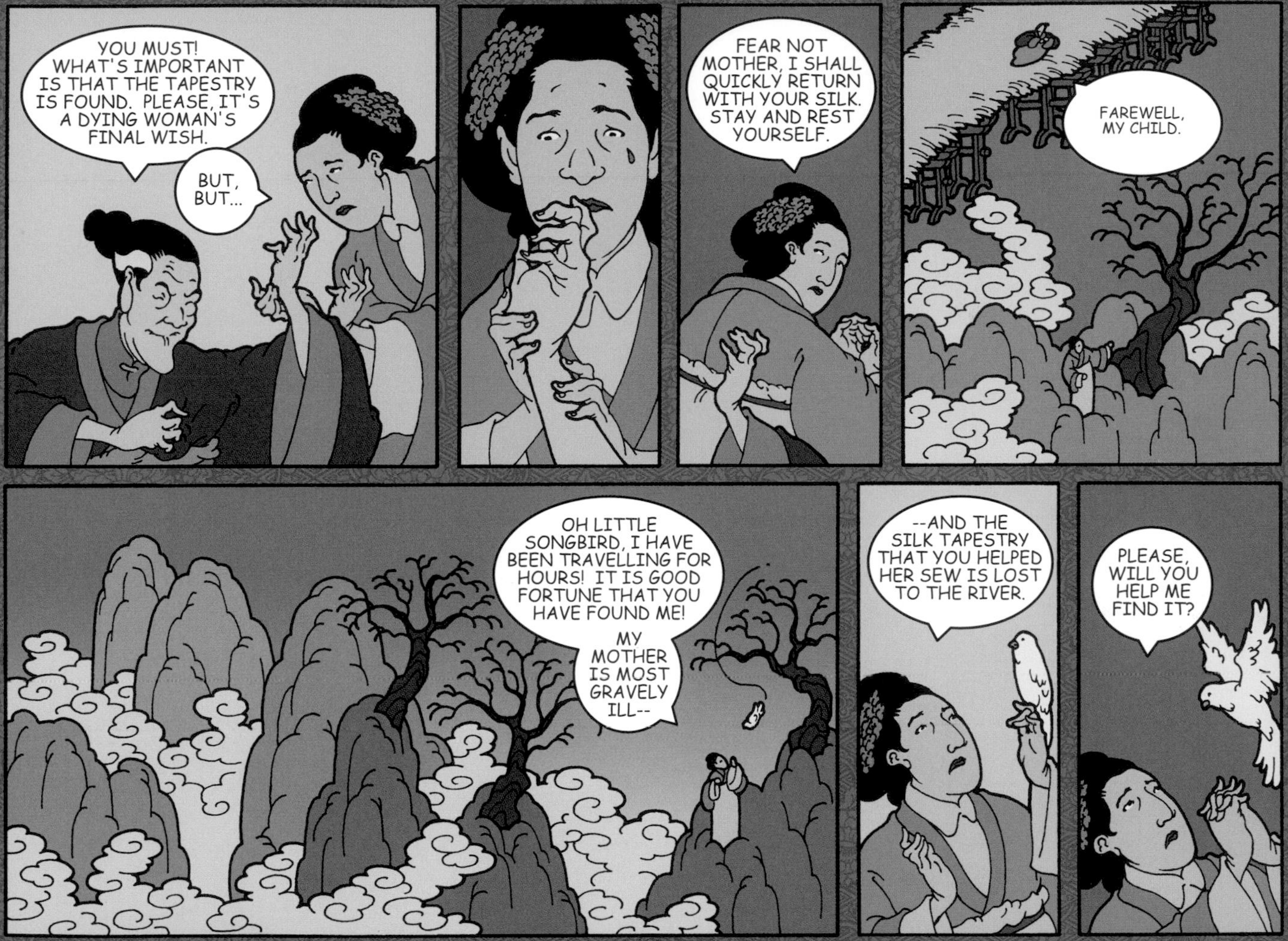
YOU MUST! WHAT'S IMPORTANT IS THAT THE TAPESTRY IS FOUND. PLEASE, IT'S A DYING WOMAN'S FINAL WISH.
BUT, BUT...
FEAR NOT MOTHER, I SHALL QUICKLY RETURN WITH YOUR SILK. STAY AND REST YOURSELF.
FAREWELL, MY CHILD.
OH LITTLE SONGBIRD, I HAVE BEEN TRAVELLING FOR HOURS! IT IS GOOD FORTUNE THAT YOU HAVE FOUND ME!
MY MOTHER IS MOST GRAVELY ILL--
--AND THE SILK TAPESTRY THAT YOU HELPED HER SEW IS LOST TO THE RIVER.
PLEASE, WILL YOU HELP ME FIND IT?

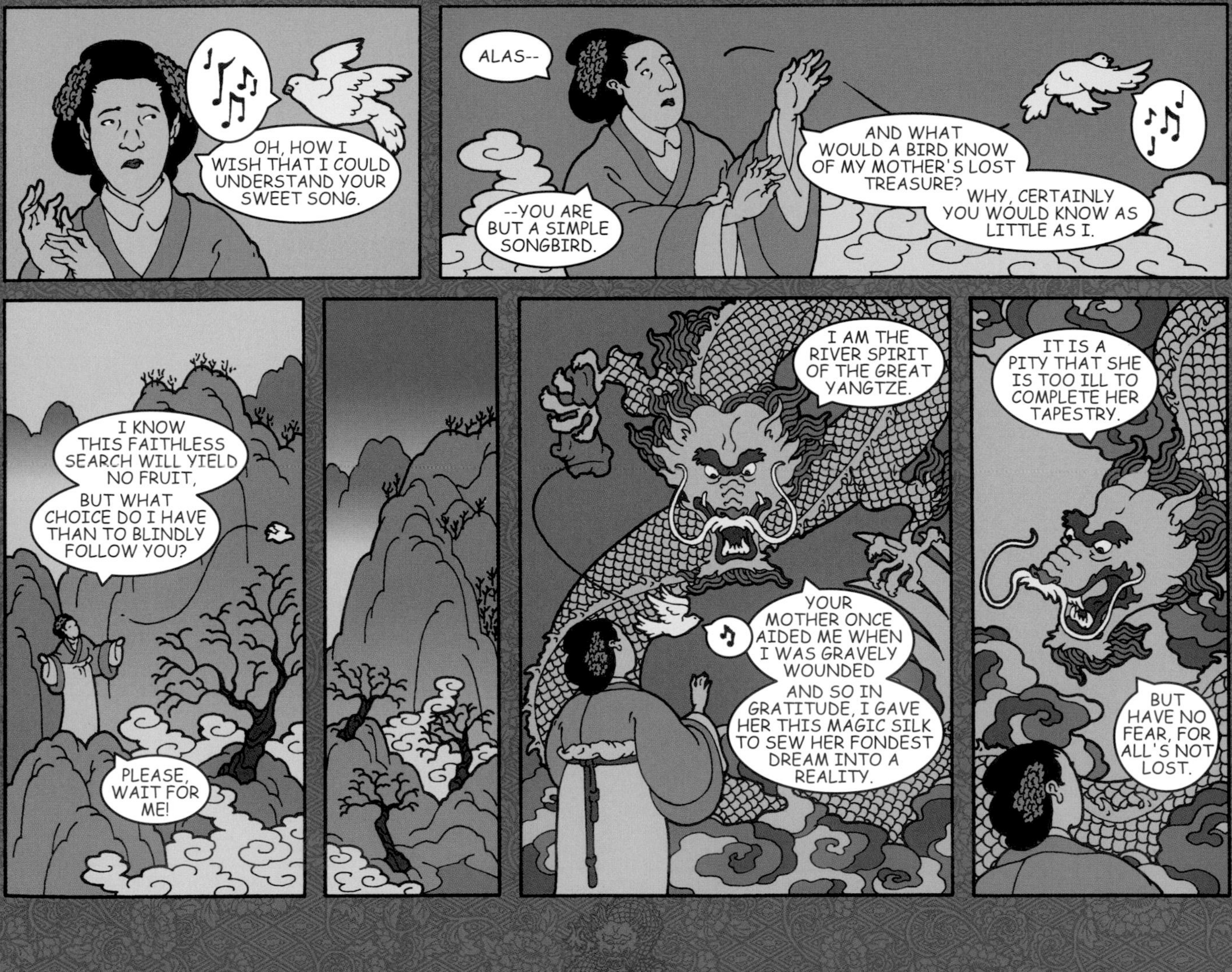

OH, HOW I WISH THAT I COULD UNDERSTAND YOUR SWEET SONG.
ALAS--
--YOU ARE BUT A SIMPLE SONGBIRD.
AND WHAT WOULD A BIRD KNOW OF MY MOTHER'S LOST TREASURE?
WHY, CERTAINLY YOU WOULD KNOW AS LITTLE AS I.
I KNOW THIS FAITHLESS SEARCH WILL YIELD NO FRUIT,
BUT WHAT CHOICE DO I HAVE THAN TO BLINDLY FOLLOW YOU?
PLEASE, WAIT FOR ME!
I AM THE RIVER SPIRIT OF THE GREAT YANGTZE.
YOUR MOTHER ONCE AIDED ME WHEN I WAS GRAVELY WOUNDED
AND SO IN GRATITUDE, I GAVE HER THIS MAGIC SILK TO SEW HER FONDEST DREAM INTO A REALITY.
IT IS A PITY THAT SHE IS TOO ILL TO COMPLETE HER TAPESTRY.
BUT HAVE NO FEAR, FOR ALL'S NOT LOST.

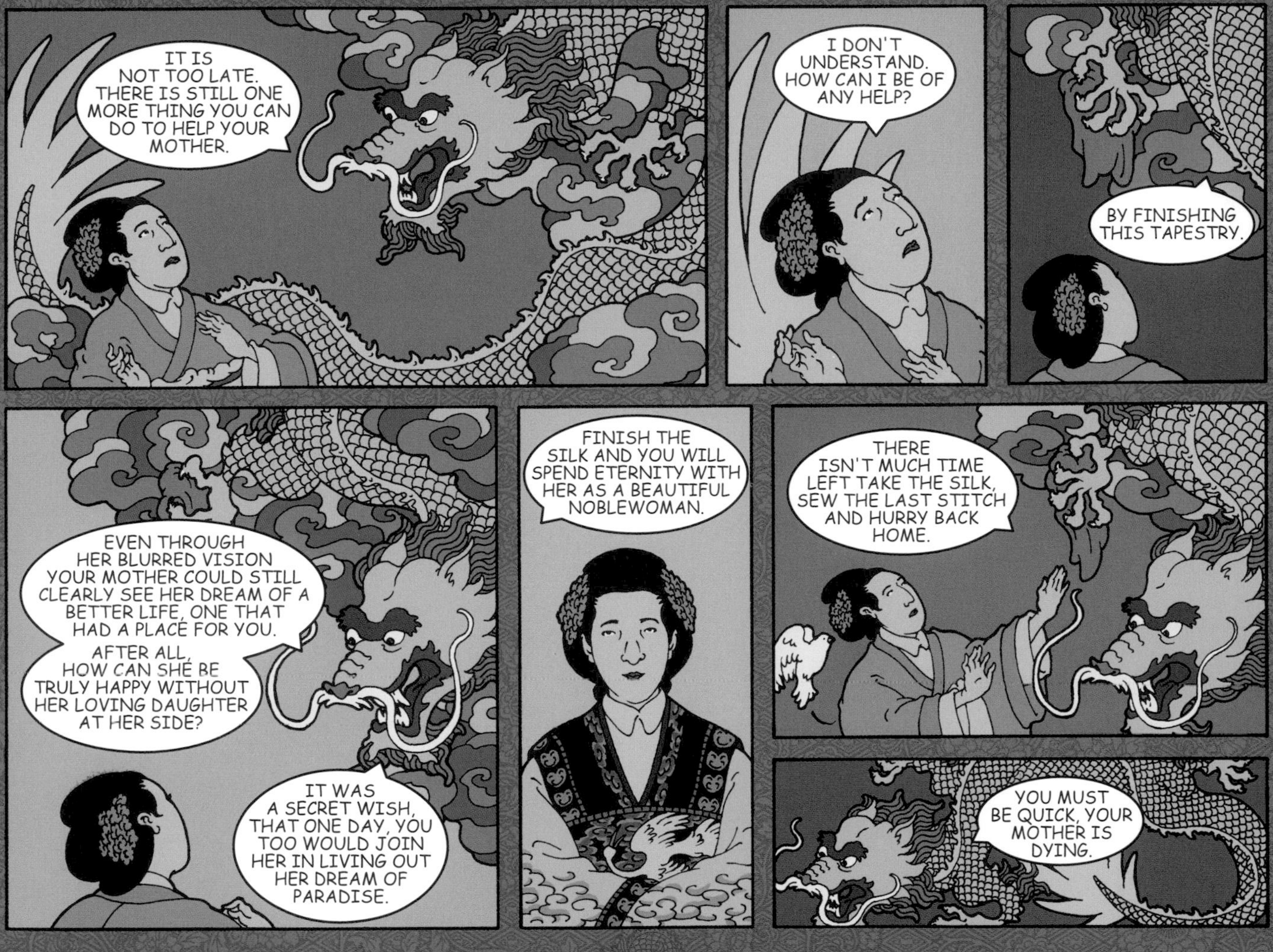
IT IS NOT TOO LATE. THERE IS STILL ONE MORE THING YOU CAN DO TO HELP YOUR MOTHER.
I DON'T UNDERSTAND. HOW CAN I BE OF ANY HELP?
BY FINISHING THIS TAPESTRY.
EVEN THROUGH HER BLURRED VISION YOUR MOTHER COULD STILL CLEARLY SEE HER DREAM OF A BETTER LIFE, ONE THAT HAD A PLACE FOR YOU.
AFTER ALL, HOW CAN SHE BE TRULY HAPPY WITHOUT HER LOVING DAUGHTER AT HER SIDE?
IT WAS A SECRET WISH, THAT ONE DAY, YOU TOO WOULD JOIN HER IN LIVING OUT HER DREAM OF PARADISE.
FINISH THE SILK AND YOU WILL SPEND ETERNITY WITH HER AS A BEAUTIFUL NOBLEWOMAN.
THERE ISN'T MUCH TIME LEFT TAKE THE SILK, SEW THE LAST STITCH AND HURRY BACK HOME.
YOU MUST BE QUICK, YOUR MOTHER IS DYING.

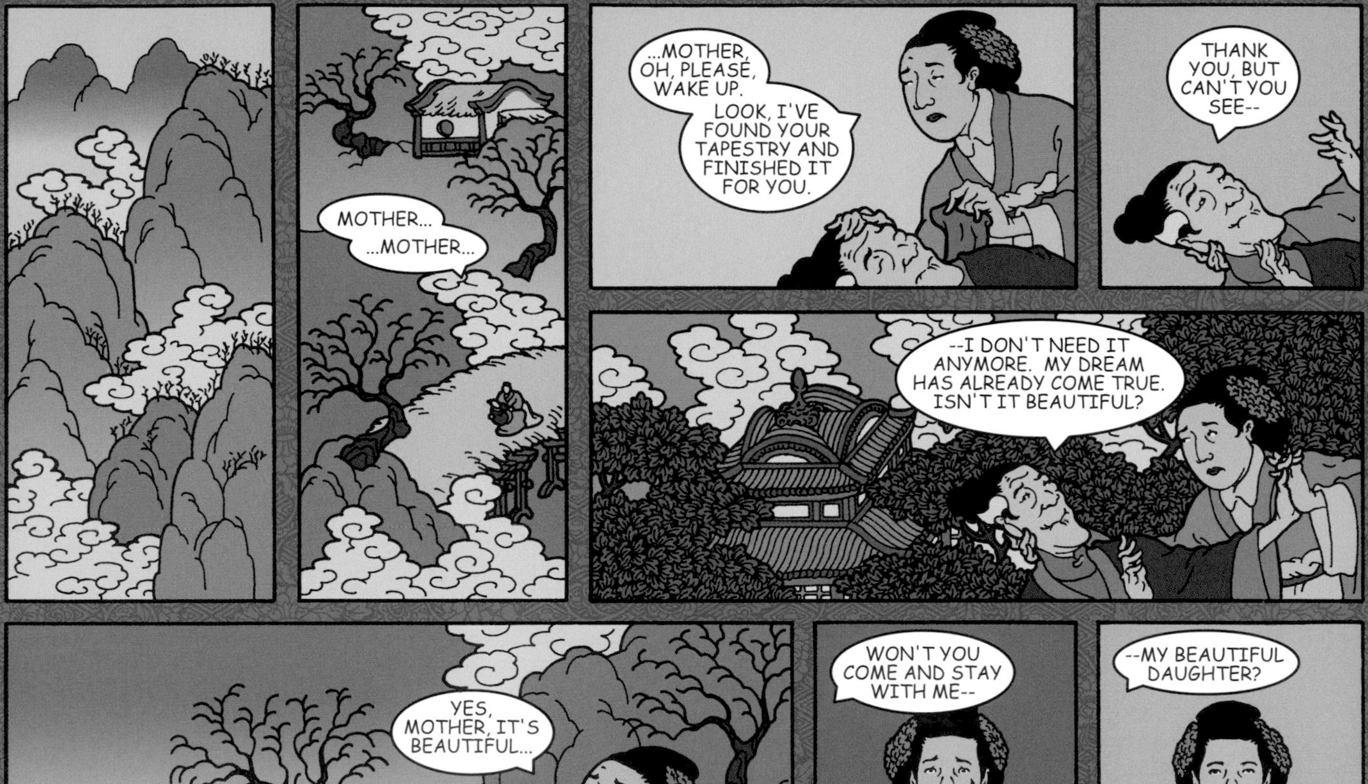
MOTHER...
...MOTHER...
...MOTHER, OH, PLEASE, WAKE UP.
LOOK, I'VE FOUND YOUR TAPESTRY AND FINISHED IT FOR YOU.
THANK YOU, BUT CAN'T YOU SEE--
--I DON'T NEED IT ANYMORE. MY DREAM HAS ALREADY COME TRUE. ISN'T IT BEAUTIFUL?
YES, MOTHER, IT'S BEAUTIFUL...
WON'T YOU COME AND STAY WITH ME--
--MY BEAUTIFUL DAUGHTER?

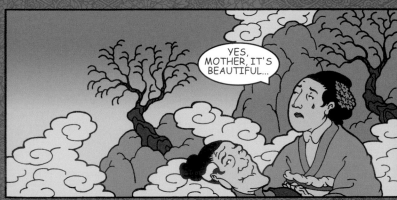

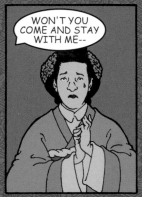

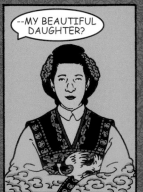

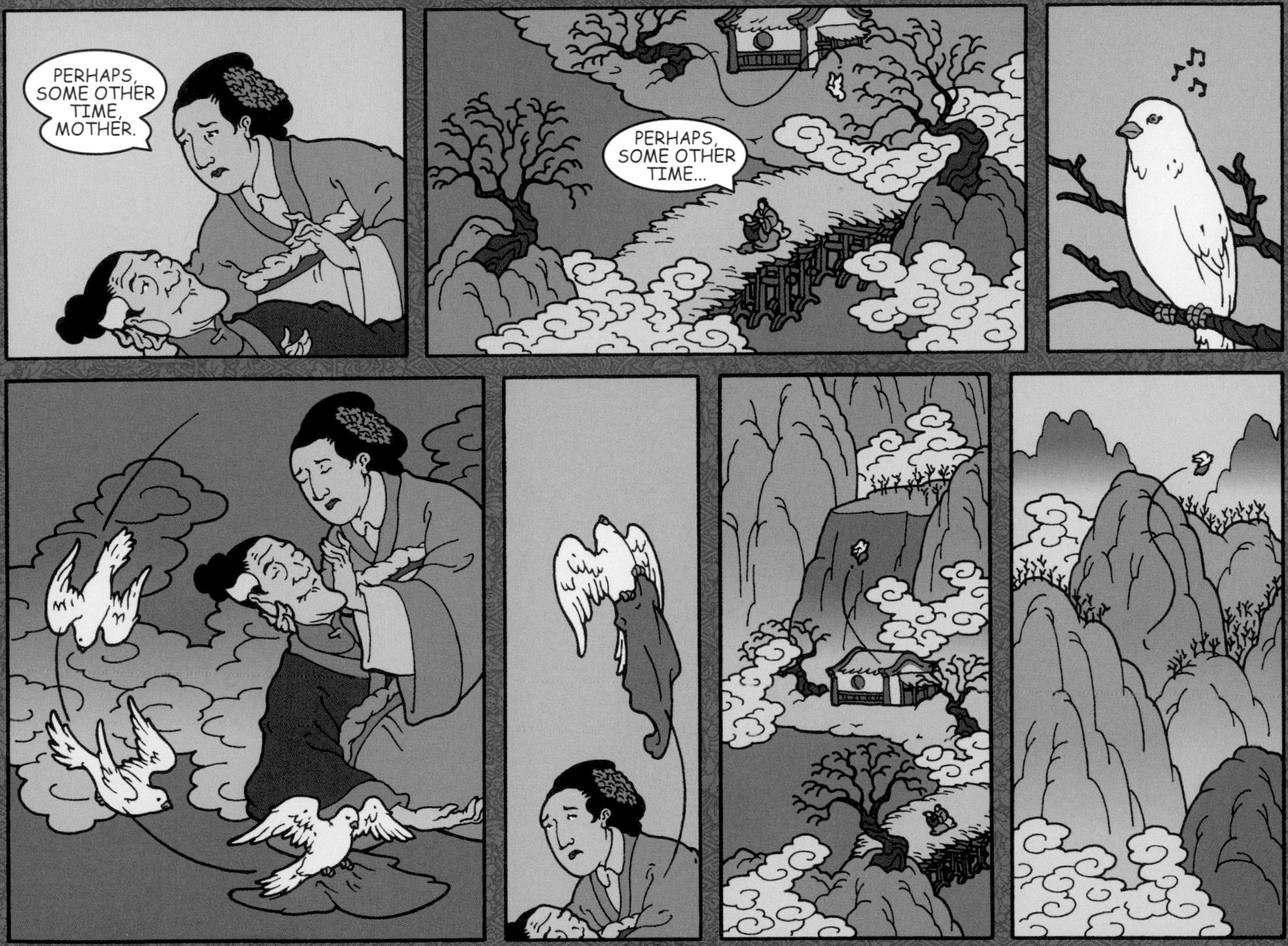
PERHAPS, SOME OTHER TIME, MOTHER.
PERHAPS, SOME OTHER TIME...

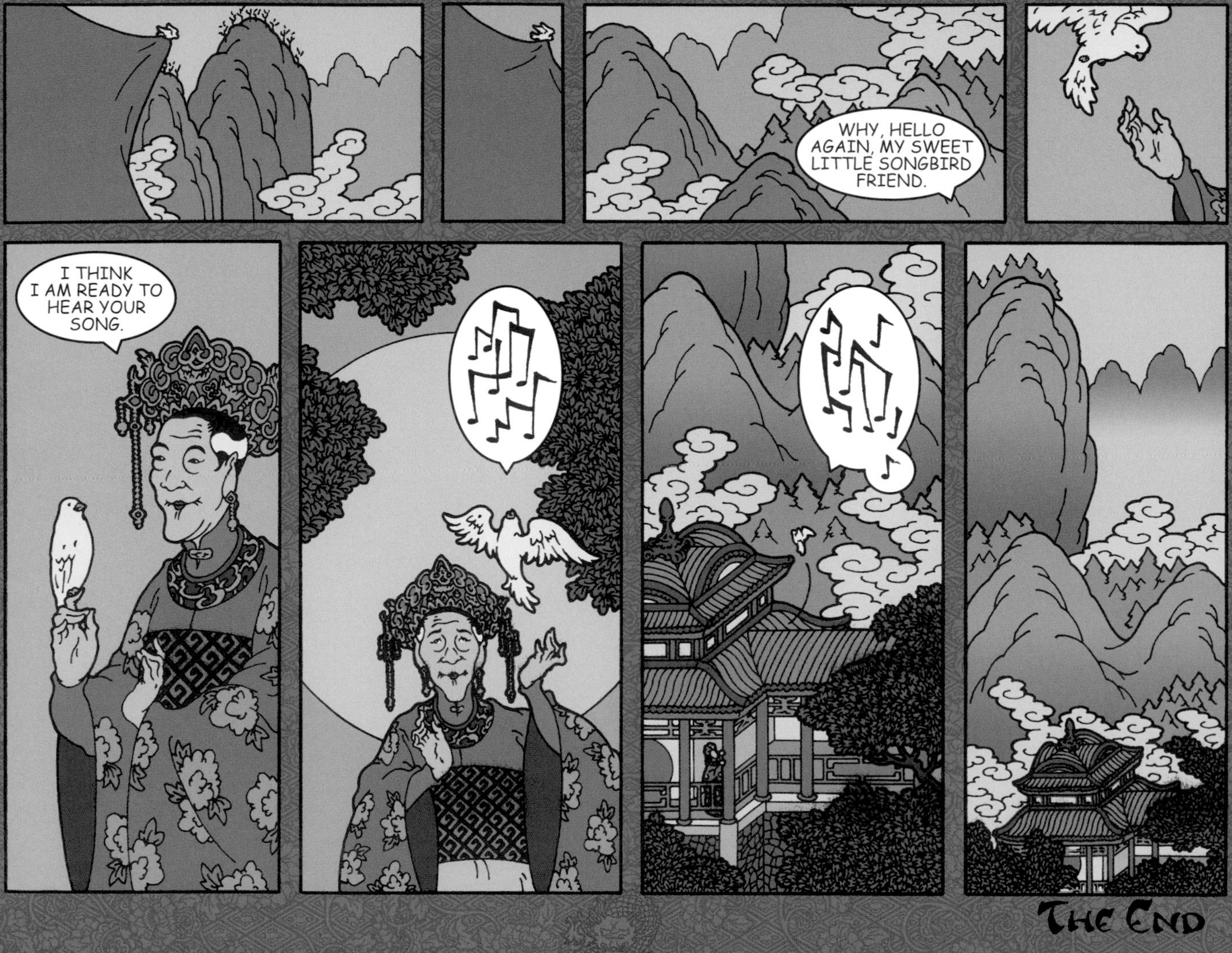
WHY, HELLO AGAIN, MY SWEET LITTLE SONGBIRD FRIEND.
I THINK I AM READY TO HEAR YOUR SONG.
THE END

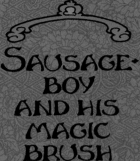

SAUSAGE-BOY AND HIS MAGIC BRUSH

ONCE UPON A TIME--

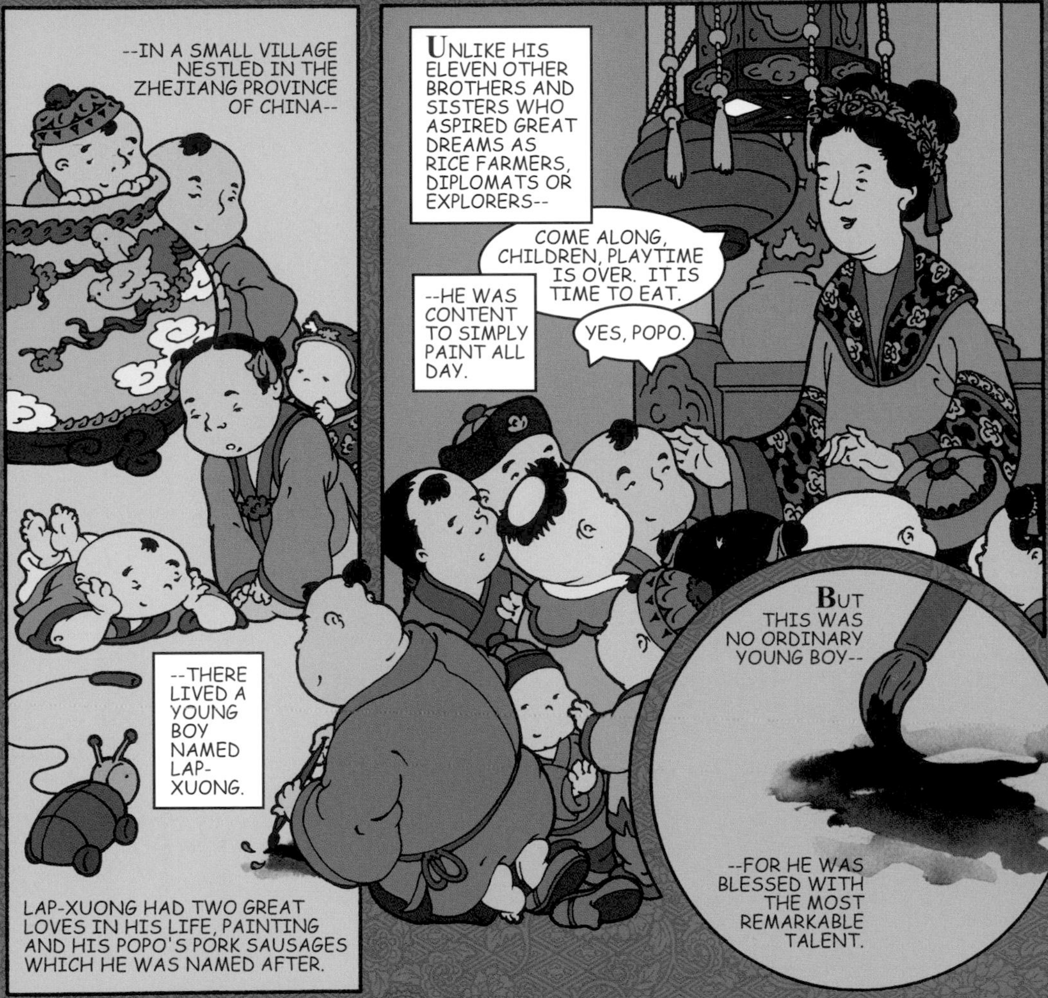
--IN A SMALL VILLAGE NESTLED IN THE ZHEJIANG PROVINCE OF CHINA--
--THERE LIVED A YOUNG BOY NAMED LAP-XUONG.
LAP-XUONG HAD TWO GREAT LOVES IN HIS LIFE, PAINTING AND HIS POPO'S PORK SAUSAGES WHICH HE WAS NAMED AFTER.
UNLIKE HIS ELEVEN OTHER BROTHERS AND SISTERS WHO ASPIRED GREAT DREAMS AS RICE FARMERS, DIPLOMATS OR EXPLORERS--
COME ALONG, CHILDREN, PLAYTIME IS OVER. IT IS TIME TO EAT.
--HE WAS CONTENT TO SIMPLY PAINT ALL DAY.
YES, POPO.
BUT THIS WAS NO ORDINARY YOUNG BOY--
--FOR HE WAS BLESSED WITH THE MOST REMARKABLE TALENT.

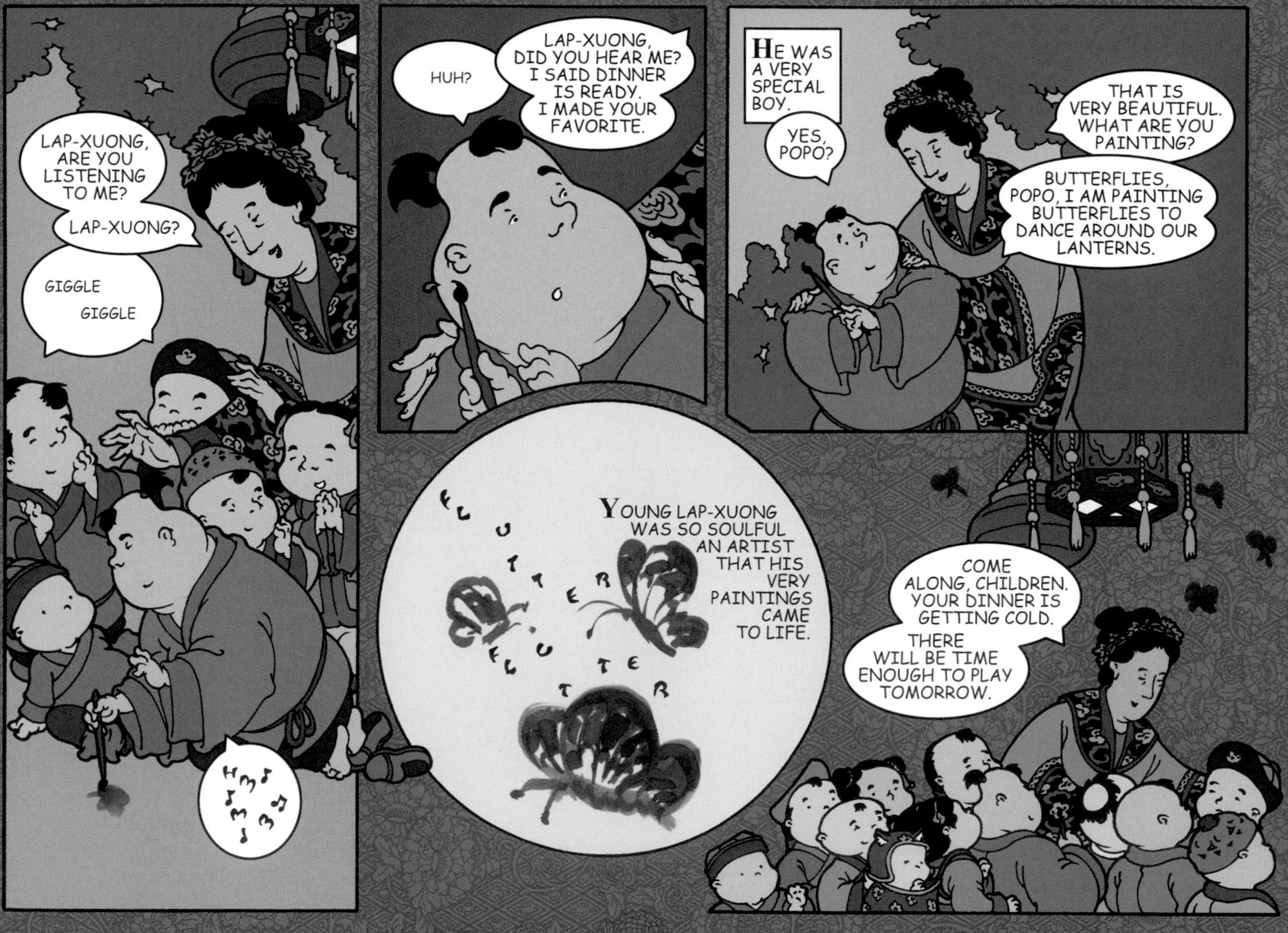
LAP-XUONG, ARE YOU LISTENING TO ME?
LAP-XUONG?
GIGGLE GIGGLE
HUH?
LAP-XUONG, DID YOU HEAR ME? I SAID DINNER IS READY. I MADE YOUR FAVORITE.
HE WAS A VERY SPECIAL BOY.
YES, POPO?
THAT IS VERY BEAUTIFUL. WHAT ARE YOU PAINTING?
BUTTERFLIES, POPO, I AM PAINTING BUTTERFLIES TO DANCE AROUND OUR LANTERNS.
FLUTTER FLUTTER
YOUNG LAP-XUONG WAS SO SOULFUL AN ARTIST THAT HIS VERY PAINTINGS CAME TO LIFE.
COME ALONG, CHILDREN. YOUR DINNER IS GETTING COLD.
THERE WILL BE TIME ENOUGH TO PLAY TOMORROW.

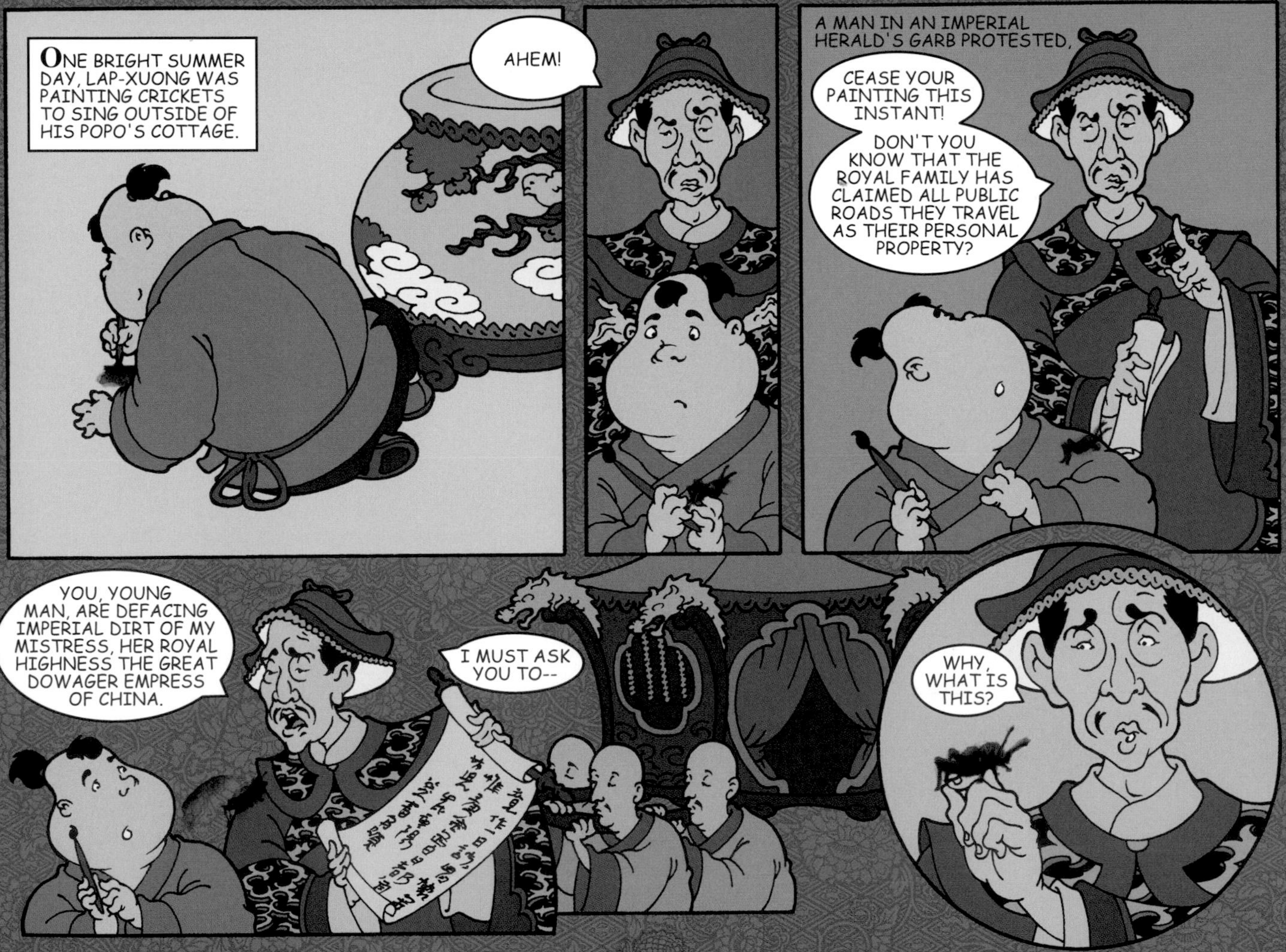
ONE BRIGHT SUMMER DAY, LAP-XUONG WAS PAINTING CRICKETS TO SING OUTSIDE OF HIS POPO'S COTTAGE.
AHEM!
A MAN IN AN IMPERIAL HERALD'S GARB PROTESTED,
CEASE YOUR PAINTING THIS INSTANT!
DON'T YOU KNOW THAT THE ROYAL FAMILY HAS CLAIMED ALL PUBLIC ROADS THEY TRAVEL AS THEIR PERSONAL PROPERTY?
YOU, YOUNG MAN, ARE DEFACING IMPERIAL DIRT OF MY MISTRESS, HER ROYAL HIGHNESS THE GREAT DOWAGER EMPRESS OF CHINA.
I MUST ASK YOU TO--
WHY, WHAT IS THIS?

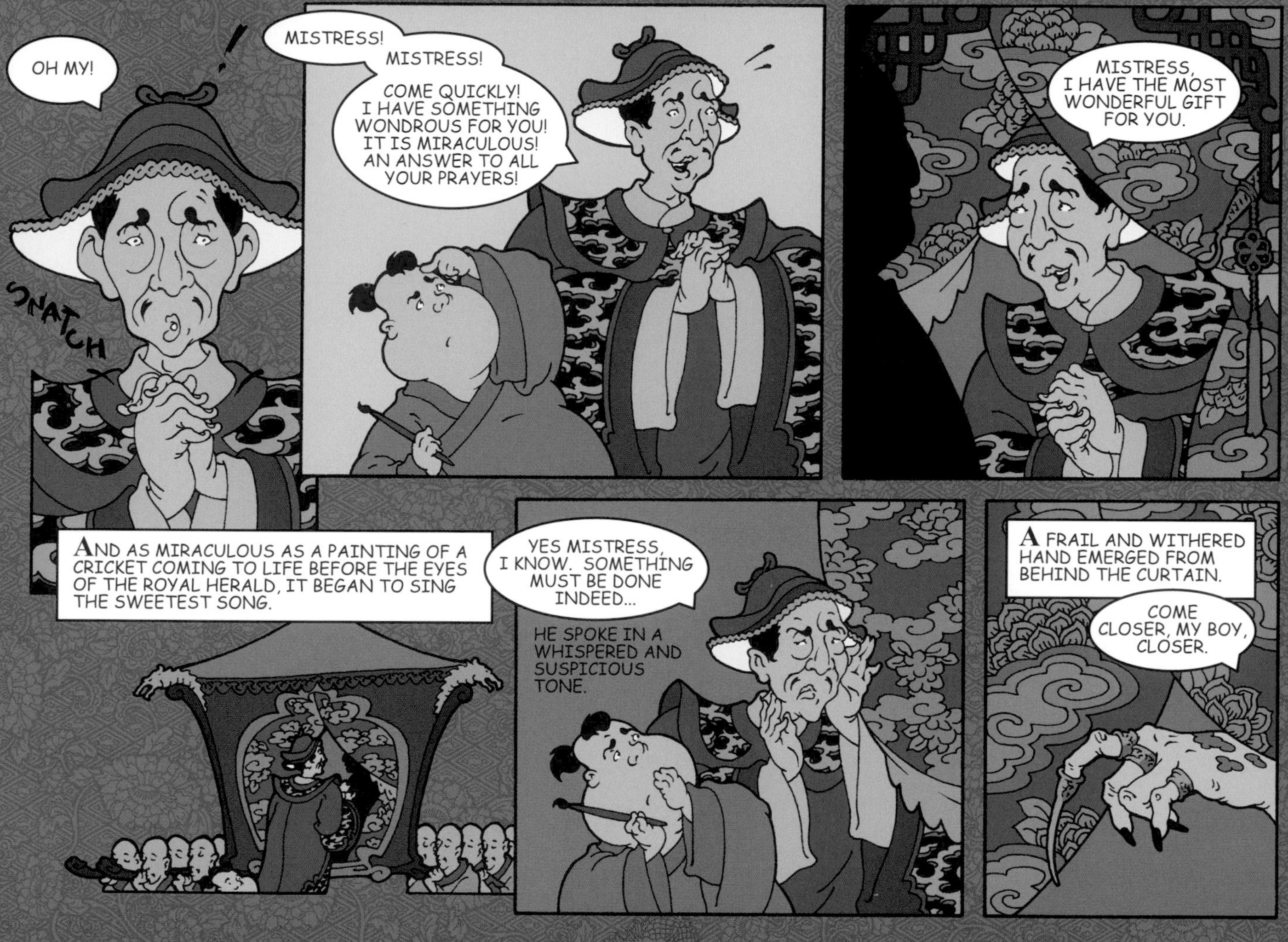
OH MY!
SNATCH
MISTRESS!
MISTRESS!
COME QUICKLY! I HAVE SOMETHING WONDROUS FOR YOU! IT IS MIRACULOUS! AN ANSWER TO ALL YOUR PRAYERS!
MISTRESS, I HAVE THE MOST WONDERFUL GIFT FOR YOU.
AND AS MIRACULOUS AS A PAINTING OF A CRICKET COMING TO LIFE BEFORE THE EYES OF THE ROYAL HERALD, IT BEGAN TO SING THE SWEETEST SONG.
YES MISTRESS, I KNOW. SOMETHING MUST BE DONE INDEED...
HE SPOKE IN A WHISPERED AND SUSPICIOUS TONE.
A FRAIL AND WITHERED HAND EMERGED FROM BEHIND THE CURTAIN.
COME CLOSER, MY BOY, CLOSER.

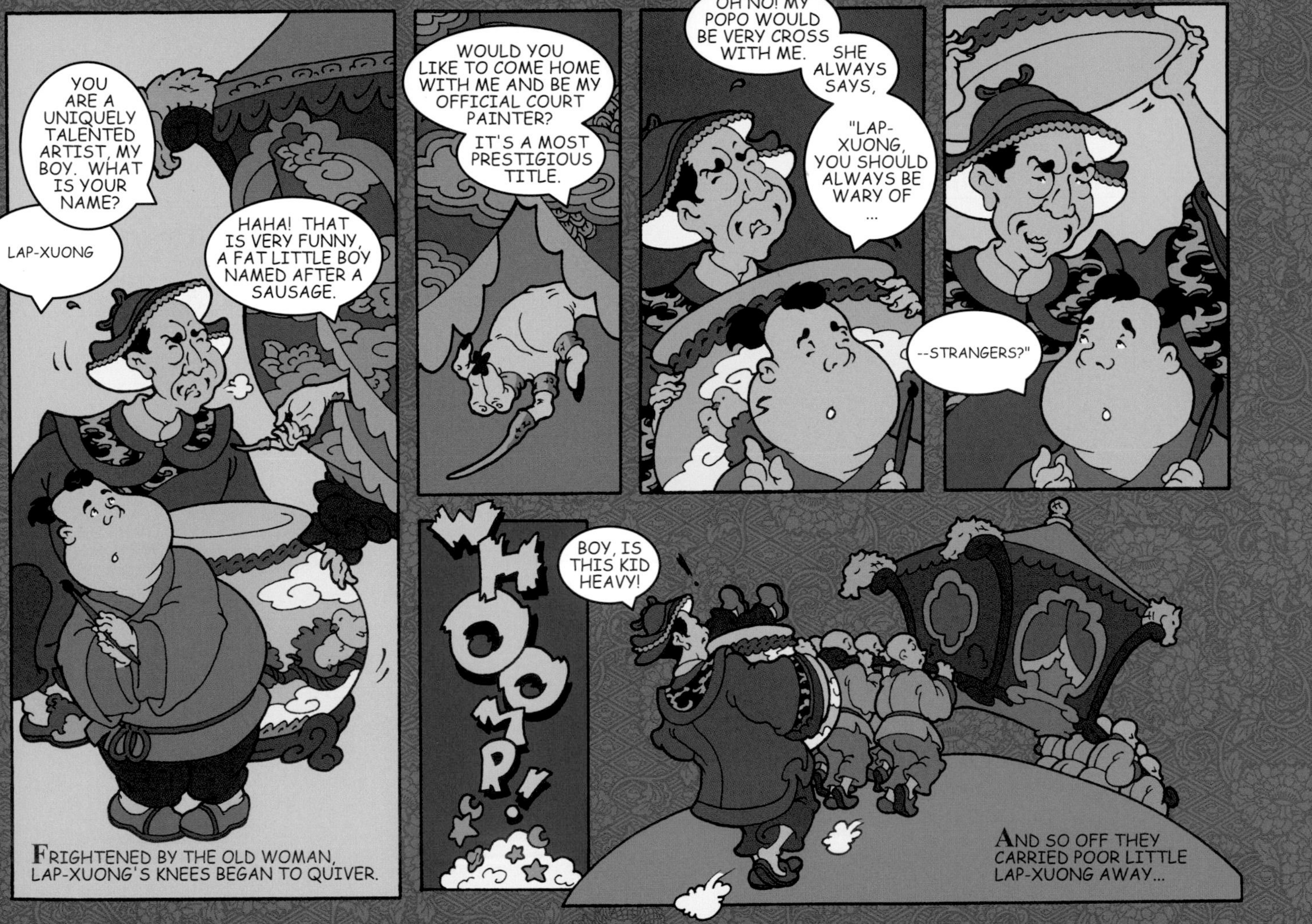
YOU ARE A UNIQUELY TALENTED ARTIST, MY BOY. WHAT IS YOUR NAME?
LAP-XUONG
HAHA! THAT IS VERY FUNNY, A FAT LITTLE BOY NAMED AFTER A SAUSAGE.
FRIGHTENED BY THE OLD WOMAN, LAP-XUONG'S KNEES BEGAN TO QUIVER.
WOULD YOU LIKE TO COME HOME WITH ME AND BE MY OFFICIAL COURT PAINTER?
IT'S A MOST PRESTIGIOUS TITLE.
OH NO! MY POPO WOULD BE VERY CROSS WITH ME.
SHE ALWAYS SAYS,
"LAP-XUONG, YOU SHOULD ALWAYS BE WARY OF ...
--STRANGERS?"
WHOOMP!
BOY, IS THIS KID HEAVY!
AND SO OFF THEY CARRIED POOR LITTLE LAP-XUONG AWAY...

WHEN LAP-XUONG AWOKE, HE FOUND HIMSELF IN A DECADENTLY FURNISHED PALACE FILLED WITH ELABORATE POTTERY AND ORNATE CARVINGS.

IT REMINDED HIM OF HIS TOWN'S CURIO SHOP, WHICH WAS NEXT TO THE LOCAL BAKERY.

WHERE AM I?

THE NEIGHBORHOOD CURIO SHOP WAS NOT ONLY FILLED WITH BIZZARE TRINKETS BUT WAS ALSO FILLED WITH THE DELICATE AROMA OF STICKY RICE BUNS AND SWEET MUNG BEANS.

THIS MEMORY MADE POOR LAP-XUONG'S STOMACH GRUMBLE--

AHEM!

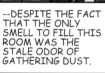

--DESPITE THE FACT THAT THE ONLY SMELL TO FILL THIS ROOM WAS THE STALE ODOR OF GATHERING DUST.

A BEJEWELED FIGURE APPEARED FROM BEHIND THE CURTAIN.

THEN, THE HERALD QUITE LOUDLY ANNOUNCED AS IF THE PALACE WAS FILLED WITH HUNDREDS OF OTHERS,

PRESENTING HER MOST LOVELY MAJESTY, QUEEN OF ALL QUEENS, HER ROYAL HIGHNESS, DOWAGER EMPRESS OF--

SILENCE!

THE OLD WOMAN THEN TURNED TO THE BEWILDERED LAP-XUONG AND ADDRESSED HIM WITH A PAINTED SMILE.

WHY, HELLO, DEAR BOY!

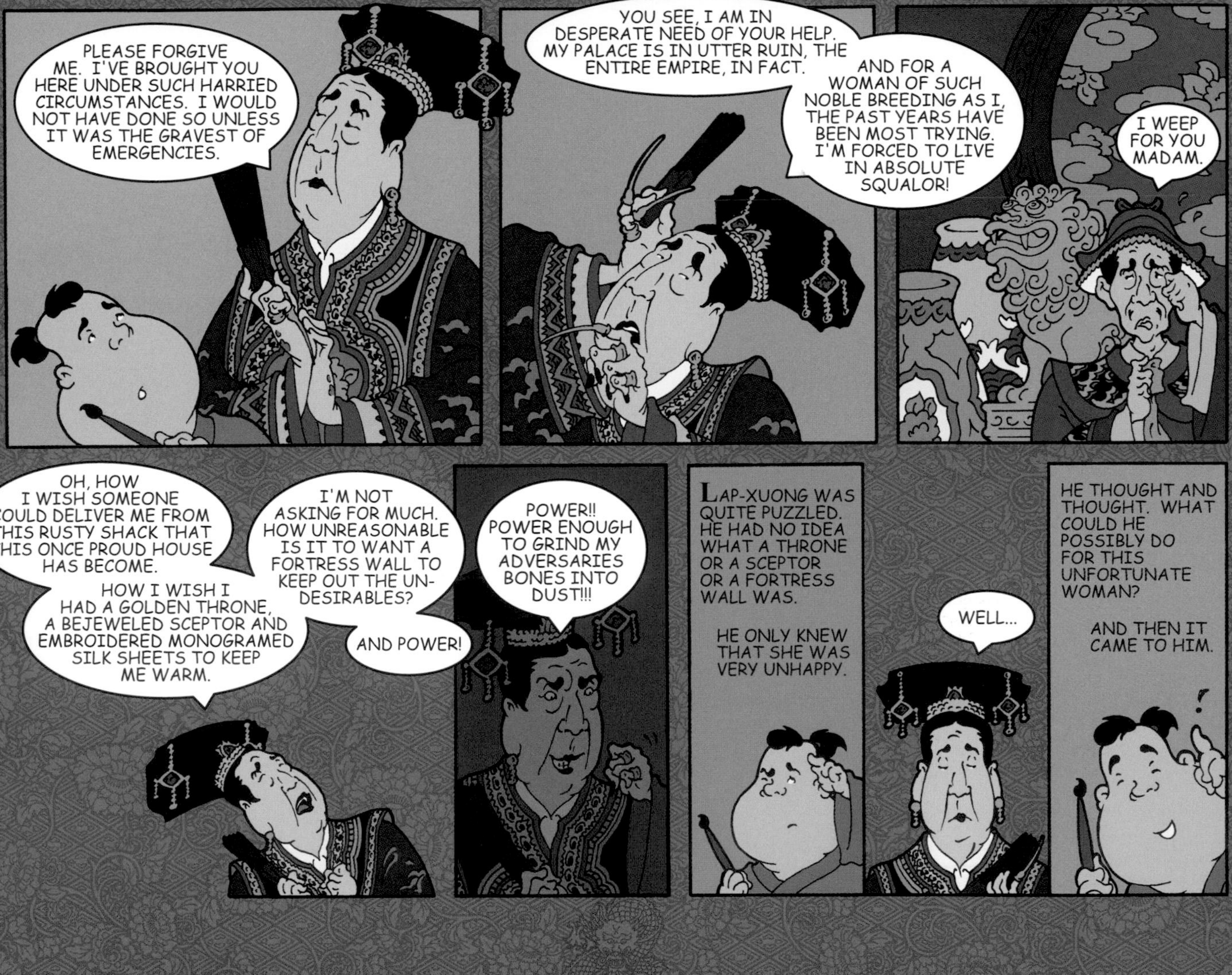
PLEASE FORGIVE ME. I'VE BROUGHT YOU HERE UNDER SUCH HARRIED CIRCUMSTANCES. I WOULD NOT HAVE DONE SO UNLESS IT WAS THE GRAVEST OF EMERGENCIES.
YOU SEE, I AM IN DESPERATE NEED OF YOUR HELP. MY PALACE IS IN UTTER RUIN, THE ENTIRE EMPIRE, IN FACT.
AND FOR A WOMAN OF SUCH NOBLE BREEDING AS I, THE PAST YEARS HAVE BEEN MOST TRYING. I'M FORCED TO LIVE IN ABSOLUTE SQUALOR!
I WEEP FOR YOU MADAM.
OH, HOW I WISH SOMEONE COULD DELIVER ME FROM THIS RUSTY SHACK THAT THIS ONCE PROUD HOUSE HAS BECOME.
HOW I WISH I HAD A GOLDEN THRONE, A BEJEWELED SCEPTOR AND EMBROIDERED MONOGRAMED SILK SHEETS TO KEEP ME WARM.
I'M NOT ASKING FOR MUCH. HOW UNREASONABLE IS IT TO WANT A FORTRESS WALL TO KEEP OUT THE UN-DESIRABLES?
AND POWER!
POWER!! POWER ENOUGH TO GRIND MY ADVERSARIES BONES INTO DUST!!!
LAP-XUONG WAS QUITE PUZZLED. HE HAD NO IDEA WHAT A THRONE OR A SCEPTOR OR A FORTRESS WALL WAS.
HE ONLY KNEW THAT SHE WAS VERY UNHAPPY.
WELL...
HE THOUGHT AND THOUGHT. WHAT COULD HE POSSIBLY DO FOR THIS UNFORTUNATE WOMAN?
AND THEN IT CAME TO HIM.
!

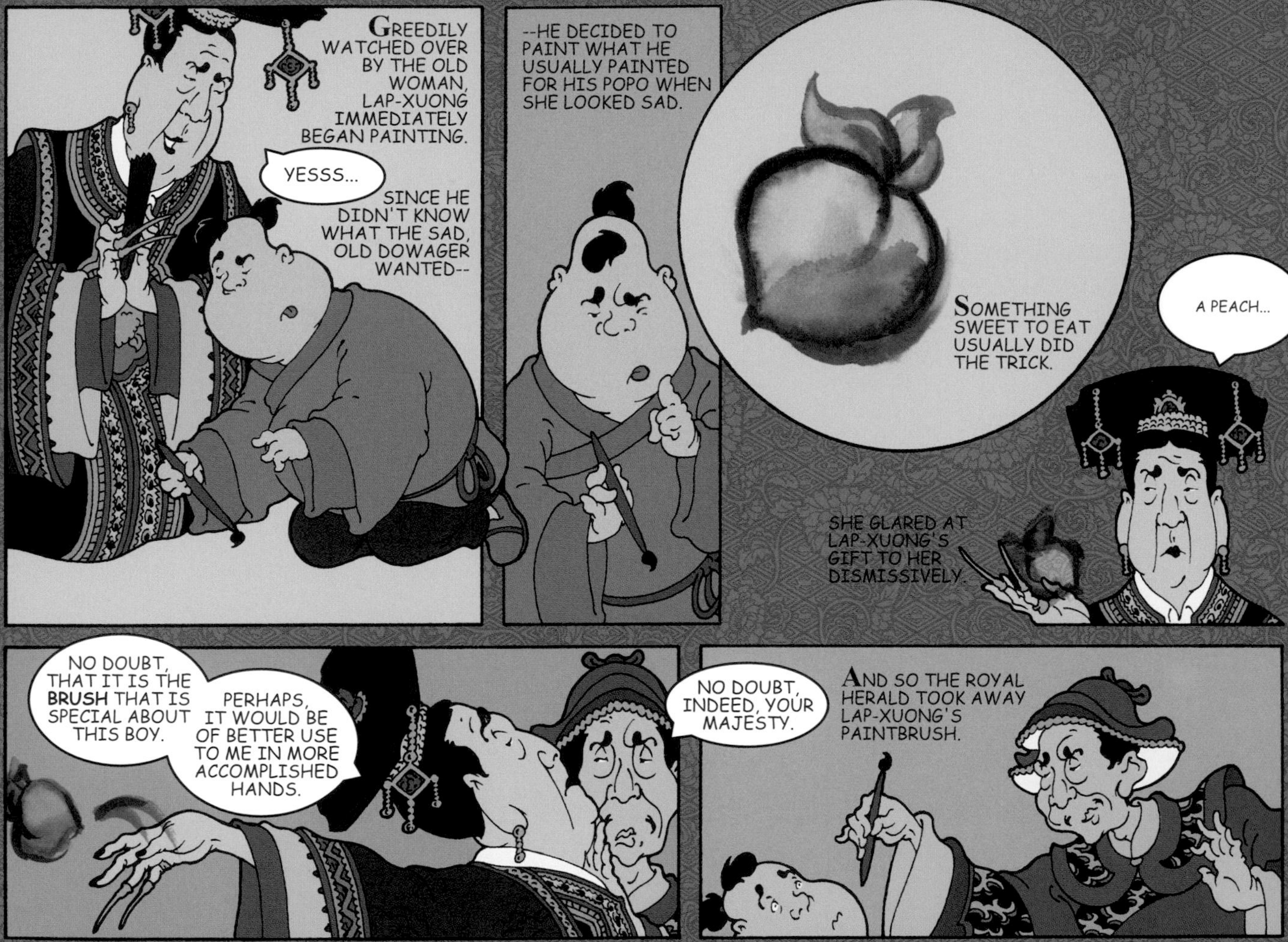
GREEDILY WATCHED OVER BY THE OLD WOMAN, LAP-XUONG IMMEDIATELY BEGAN PAINTING.
YESSS...
SINCE HE DIDN'T KNOW WHAT THE SAD, OLD DOWAGER WANTED--
--HE DECIDED TO PAINT WHAT HE USUALLY PAINTED FOR HIS POPO WHEN SHE LOOKED SAD.
SOMETHING SWEET TO EAT USUALLY DID THE TRICK.
A PEACH...
SHE GLARED AT LAP-XUONG'S GIFT TO HER DISMISSIVELY.
NO DOUBT, THAT IT IS THE **BRUSH** THAT IS SPECIAL ABOUT THIS BOY.
PERHAPS, IT WOULD BE OF BETTER USE TO ME IN MORE ACCOMPLISHED HANDS.
NO DOUBT, INDEED, YOUR MAJESTY.
AND SO THE ROYAL HERALD TOOK AWAY LAP-XUONG'S PAINTBRUSH.

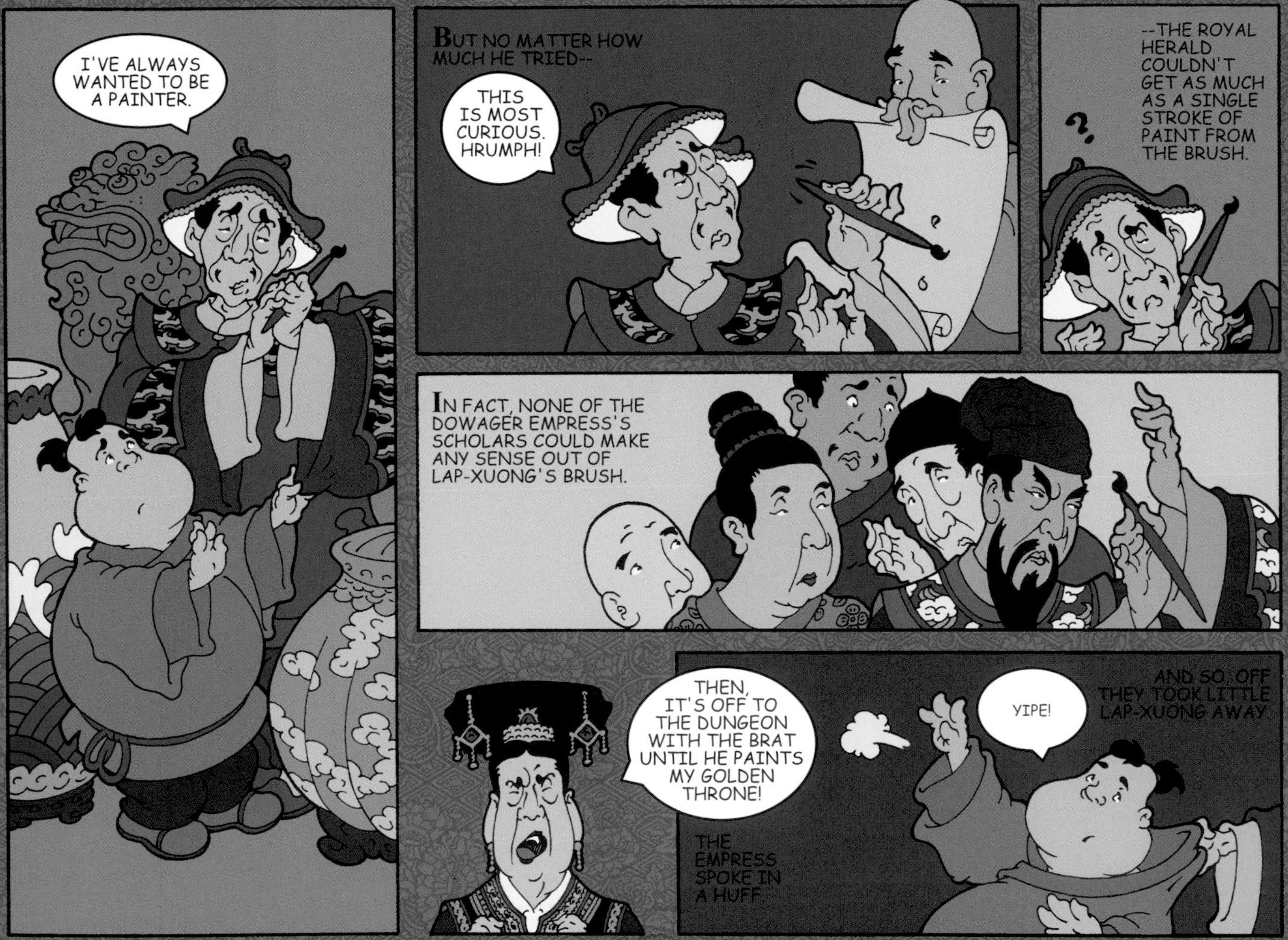
I'VE ALWAYS WANTED TO BE A PAINTER.
BUT NO MATTER HOW MUCH HE TRIED--
THIS IS MOST CURIOUS. HRUMPH!
--THE ROYAL HERALD COULDN'T GET AS MUCH AS A SINGLE STROKE OF PAINT FROM THE BRUSH.
??
IN FACT, NONE OF THE DOWAGER EMPRESS'S SCHOLARS COULD MAKE ANY SENSE OUT OF LAP-XUONG'S BRUSH.
THEN, IT'S OFF TO THE DUNGEON WITH THE BRAT UNTIL HE PAINTS MY GOLDEN THRONE!
THE EMPRESS SPOKE IN A HUFF.
AND SO, OFF THEY TOOK LITTLE LAP-XUONG AWAY.
YIPE!

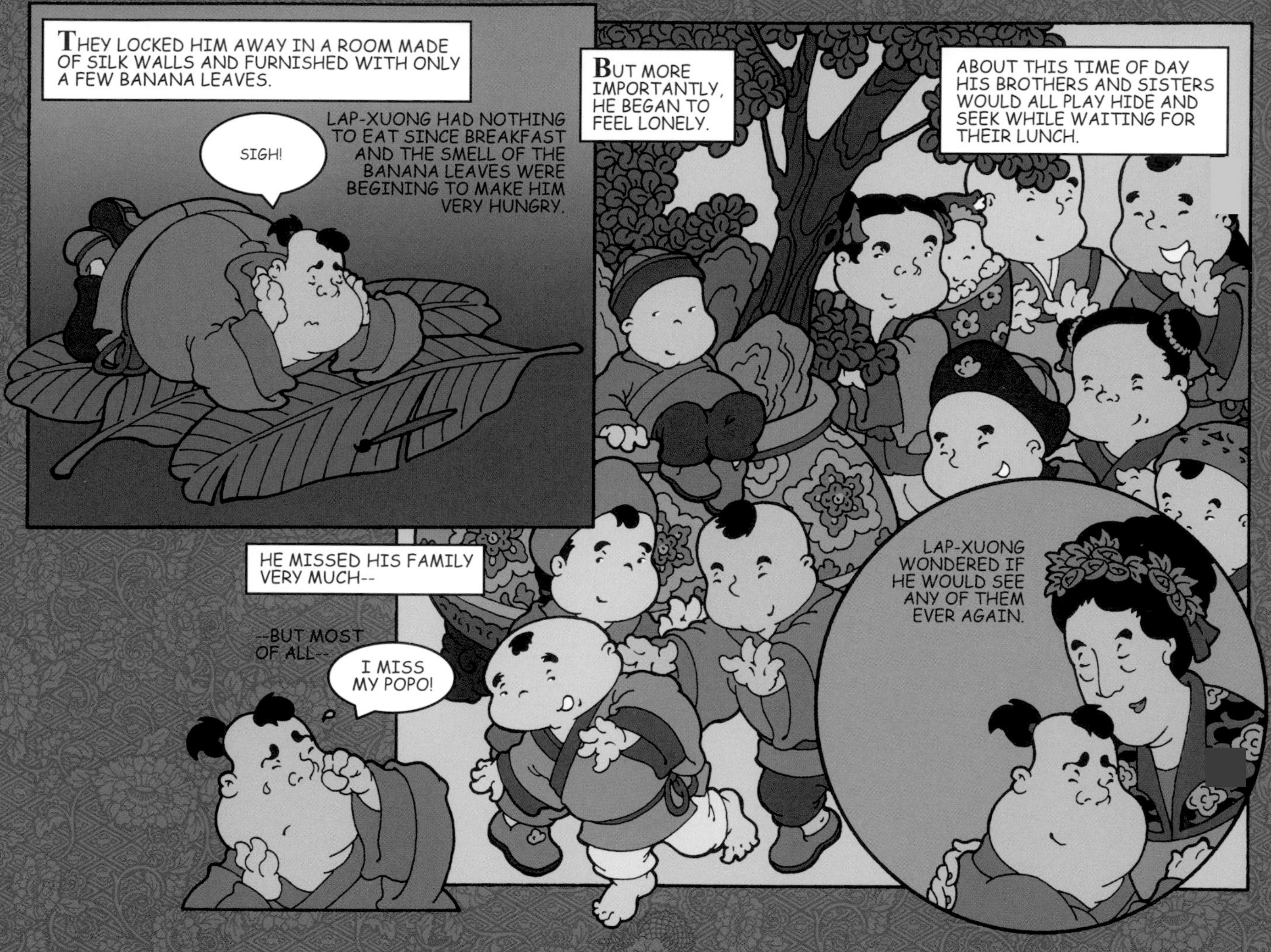
THEY LOCKED HIM AWAY IN A ROOM MADE OF SILK WALLS AND FURNISHED WITH ONLY A FEW BANANA LEAVES.
SIGH!
LAP-XUONG HAD NOTHING TO EAT SINCE BREAKFAST AND THE SMELL OF THE BANANA LEAVES WERE BEGINING TO MAKE HIM VERY HUNGRY.
BUT MORE IMPORTANTLY, HE BEGAN TO FEEL LONELY.
ABOUT THIS TIME OF DAY HIS BROTHERS AND SISTERS WOULD ALL PLAY HIDE AND SEEK WHILE WAITING FOR THEIR LUNCH.
HE MISSED HIS FAMILY VERY MUCH--
--BUT MOST OF ALL--
I MISS MY POPO!
LAP-XUONG WONDERED IF HE WOULD SEE ANY OF THEM EVER AGAIN.

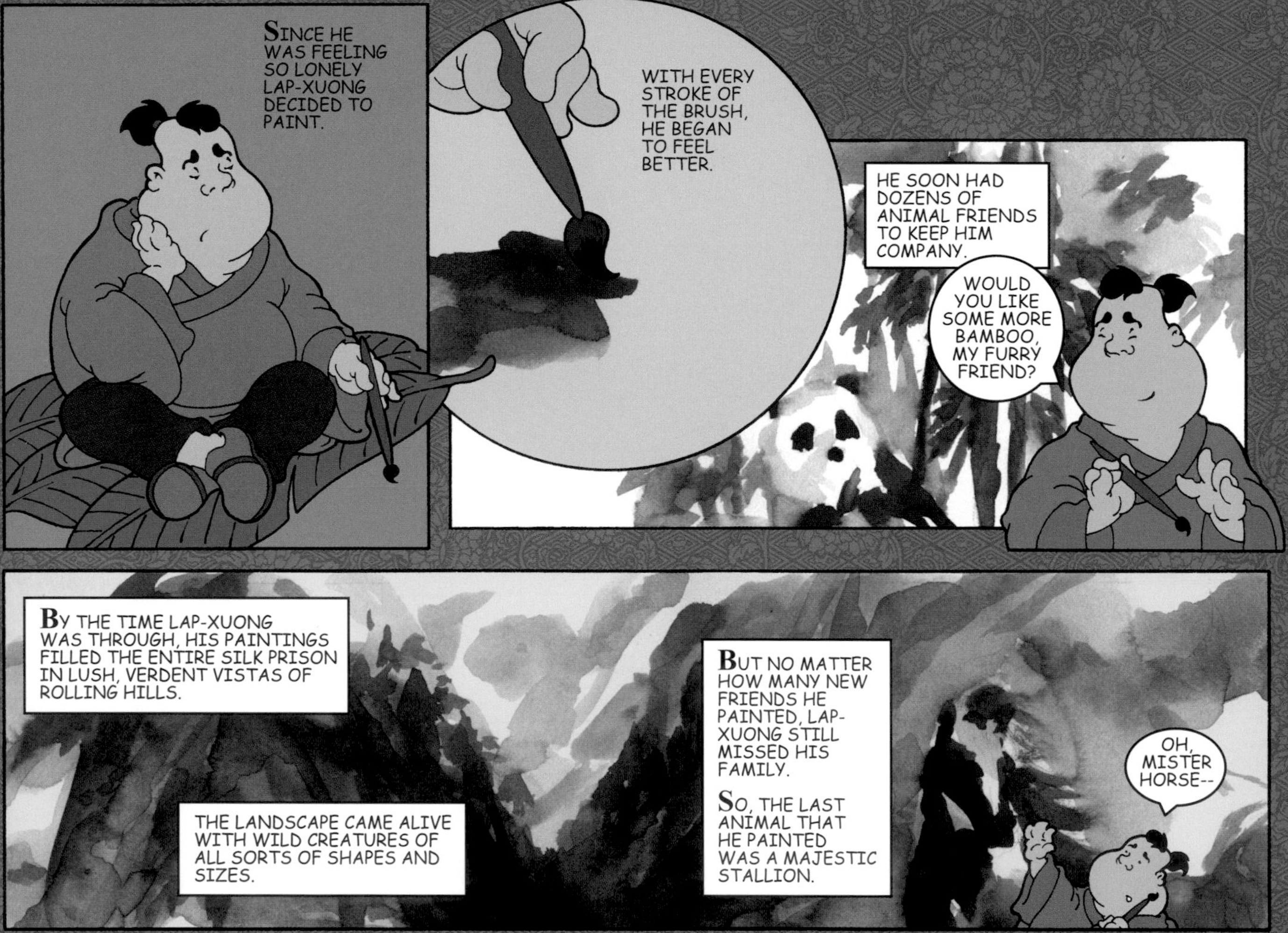
SINCE HE WAS FEELING SO LONELY LAP-XUONG DECIDED TO PAINT.
WITH EVERY STROKE OF THE BRUSH, HE BEGAN TO FEEL BETTER.
HE SOON HAD DOZENS OF ANIMAL FRIENDS TO KEEP HIM COMPANY.
WOULD YOU LIKE SOME MORE BAMBOO, MY FURRY FRIEND?
BY THE TIME LAP-XUONG WAS THROUGH, HIS PAINTINGS FILLED THE ENTIRE SILK PRISON IN LUSH, VERDENT VISTAS OF ROLLING HILLS.
THE LANDSCAPE CAME ALIVE WITH WILD CREATURES OF ALL SORTS OF SHAPES AND SIZES.
BUT NO MATTER HOW MANY NEW FRIENDS HE PAINTED, LAP-XUONG STILL MISSED HIS FAMILY.
SO, THE LAST ANIMAL THAT HE PAINTED WAS A MAJESTIC STALLION.
OH, MISTER HORSE--

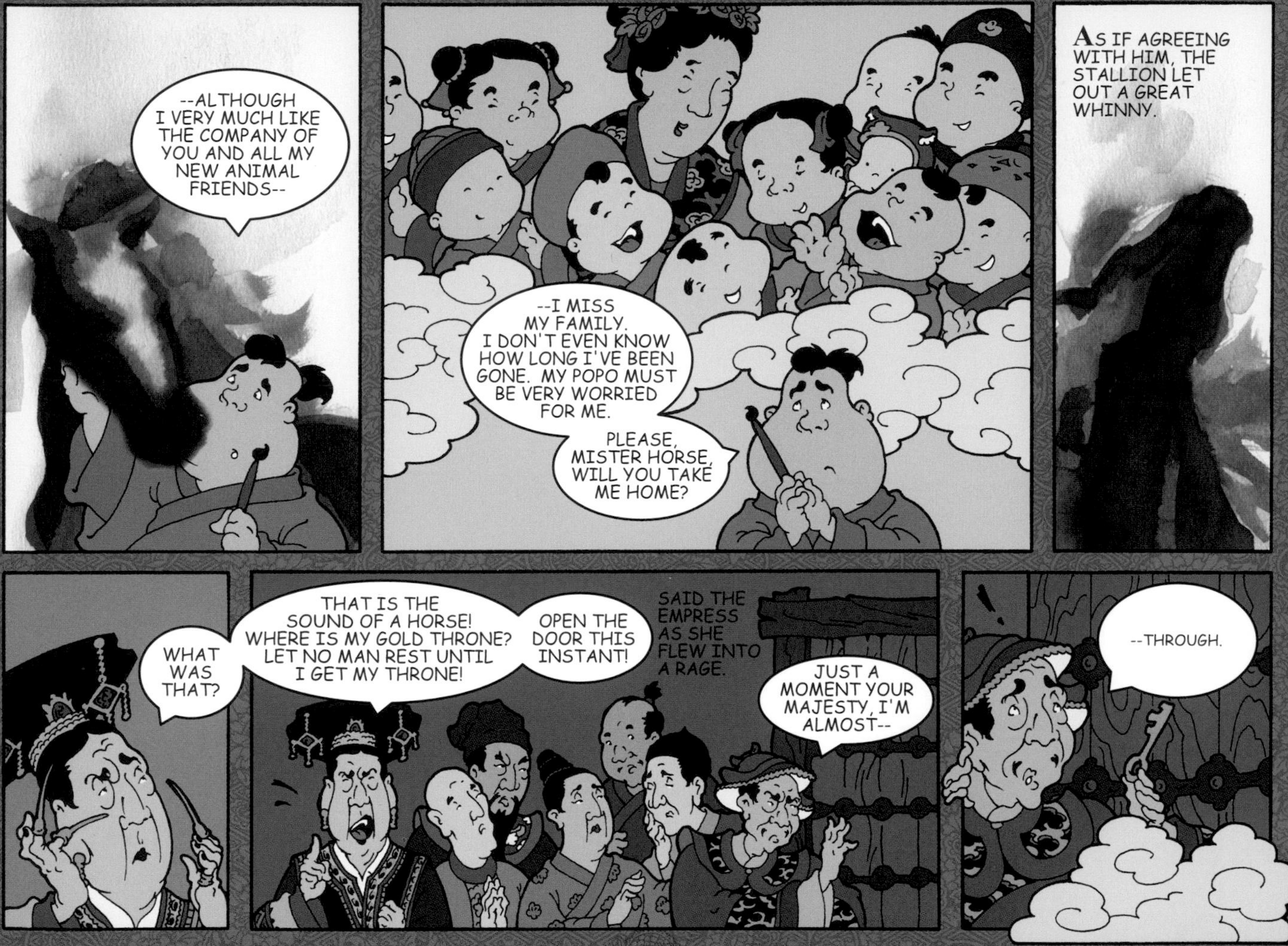
--ALTHOUGH I VERY MUCH LIKE THE COMPANY OF YOU AND ALL MY NEW ANIMAL FRIENDS--
--I MISS MY FAMILY. I DON'T EVEN KNOW HOW LONG I'VE BEEN GONE. MY POPO MUST BE VERY WORRIED FOR ME.
PLEASE, MISTER HORSE, WILL YOU TAKE ME HOME?
AS IF AGREEING WITH HIM, THE STALLION LET OUT A GREAT WHINNY.
WHAT WAS THAT?
THAT IS THE SOUND OF A HORSE! WHERE IS MY GOLD THRONE? LET NO MAN REST UNTIL I GET MY THRONE!
OPEN THE DOOR THIS INSTANT!
SAID THE EMPRESS AS SHE FLEW INTO A RAGE.
JUST A MOMENT YOUR MAJESTY, I'M ALMOST--
--THROUGH.

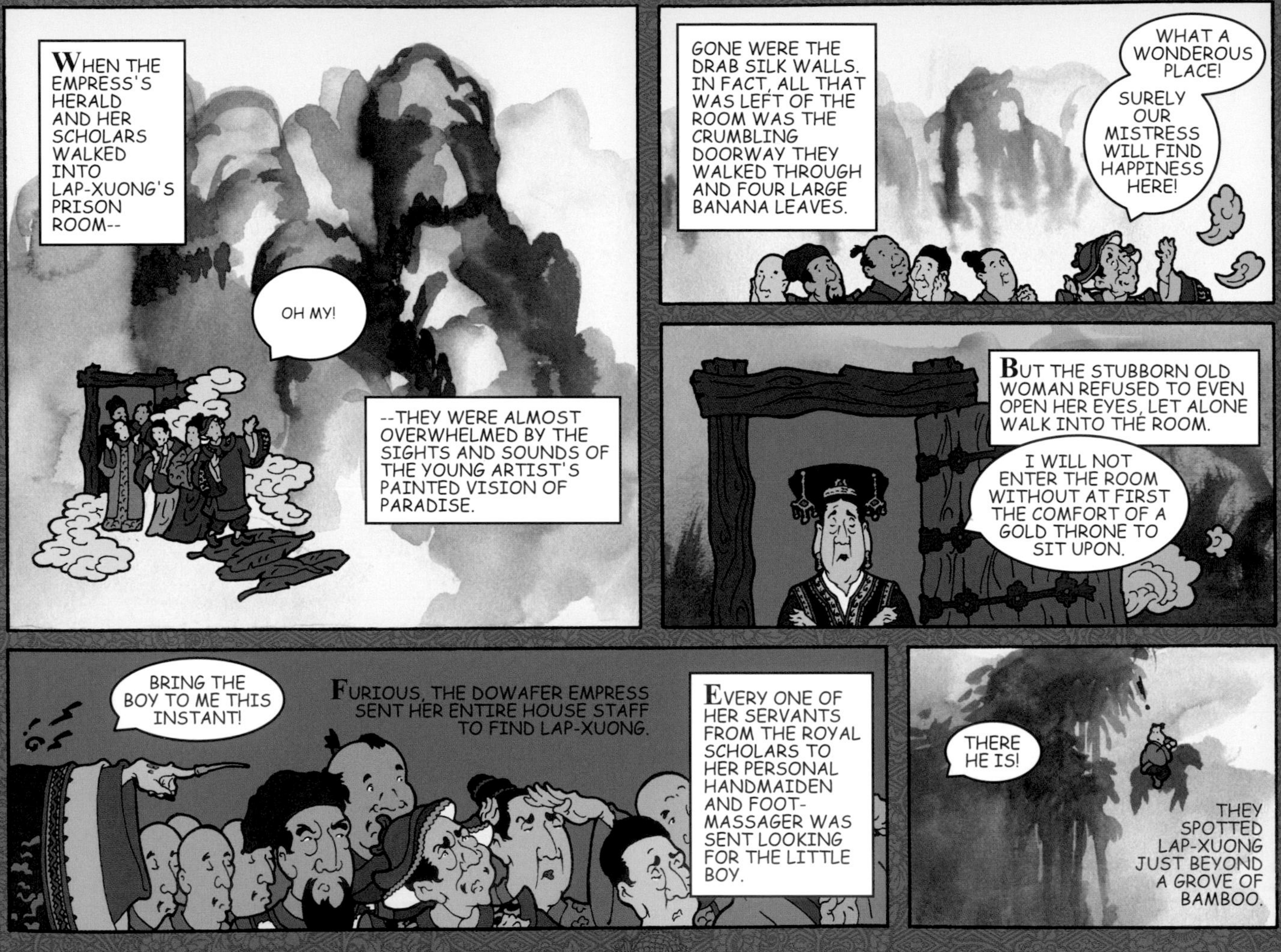
WHEN THE EMPRESS'S HERALD AND HER SCHOLARS WALKED INTO LAP-XUONG'S PRISON ROOM--
OH MY!
--THEY WERE ALMOST OVERWHELMED BY THE SIGHTS AND SOUNDS OF THE YOUNG ARTIST'S PAINTED VISION OF PARADISE.
GONE WERE THE DRAB SILK WALLS. IN FACT, ALL THAT WAS LEFT OF THE ROOM WAS THE CRUMBLING DOORWAY THEY WALKED THROUGH AND FOUR LARGE BANANA LEAVES.
WHAT A WONDEROUS PLACE!
SURELY OUR MISTRESS WILL FIND HAPPINESS HERE!
BUT THE STUBBORN OLD WOMAN REFUSED TO EVEN OPEN HER EYES, LET ALONE WALK INTO THE ROOM.
I WILL NOT ENTER THE ROOM WITHOUT AT FIRST THE COMFORT OF A GOLD THRONE TO SIT UPON.
BRING THE BOY TO ME THIS INSTANT!
FURIOUS, THE DOWAFER EMPRESS SENT HER ENTIRE HOUSE STAFF TO FIND LAP-XUONG.
EVERY ONE OF HER SERVANTS FROM THE ROYAL SCHOLARS TO HER PERSONAL HANDMAIDEN AND FOOT-MASSAGER WAS SENT LOOKING FOR THE LITTLE BOY.
THERE HE IS!
THEY SPOTTED LAP-XUONG JUST BEYOND A GROVE OF BAMBOO.

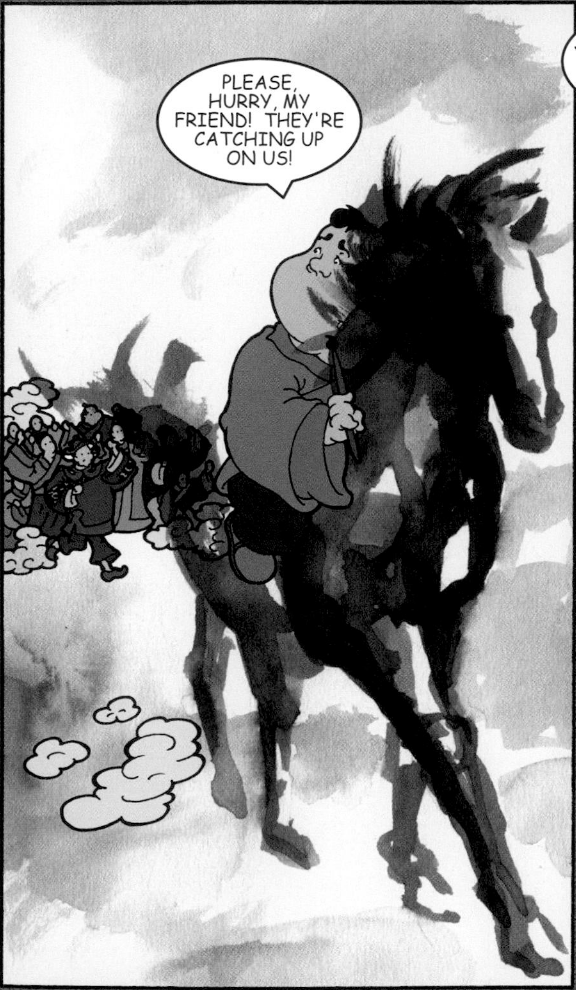
PLEASE, HURRY, MY FRIEND! THEY'RE CATCHING UP ON US!

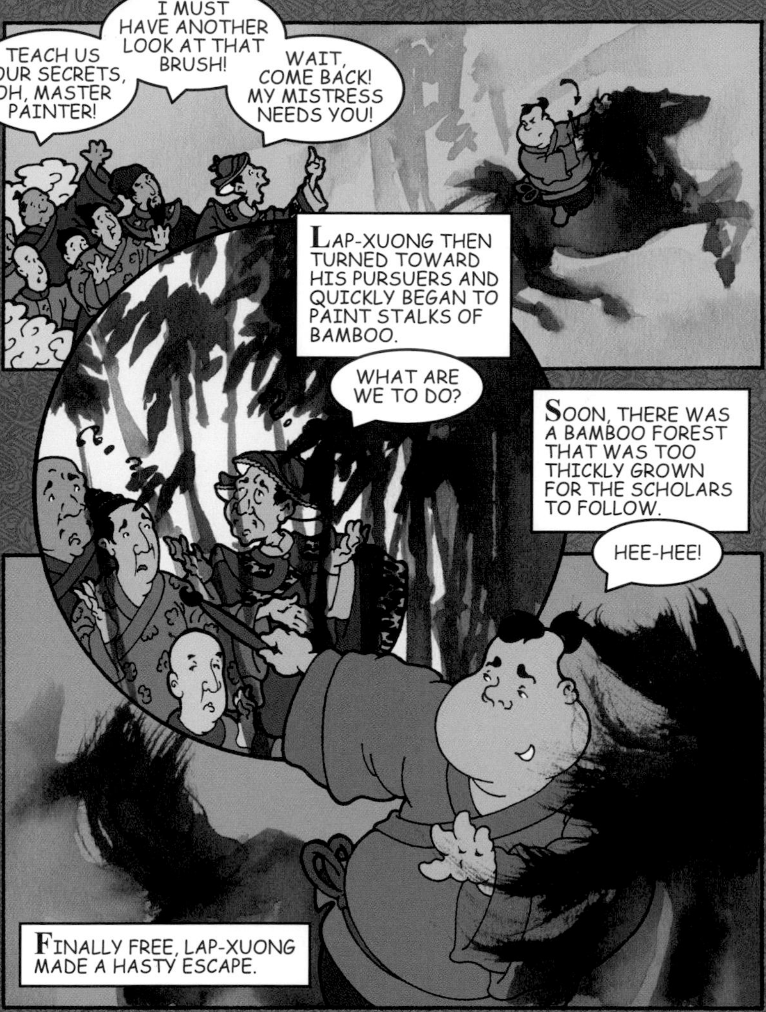
TEACH US YOUR SECRETS, OH, MASTER PAINTER!
I MUST HAVE ANOTHER LOOK AT THAT BRUSH!
WAIT, COME BACK! MY MISTRESS NEEDS YOU!
LAP-XUONG THEN TURNED TOWARD HIS PURSUERS AND QUICKLY BEGAN TO PAINT STALKS OF BAMBOO.
WHAT ARE WE TO DO?
SOON, THERE WAS A BAMBOO FOREST THAT WAS TOO THICKLY GROWN FOR THE SCHOLARS TO FOLLOW.
HEE-HEE!
FINALLY FREE, LAP-XUONG MADE A HASTY ESCAPE.

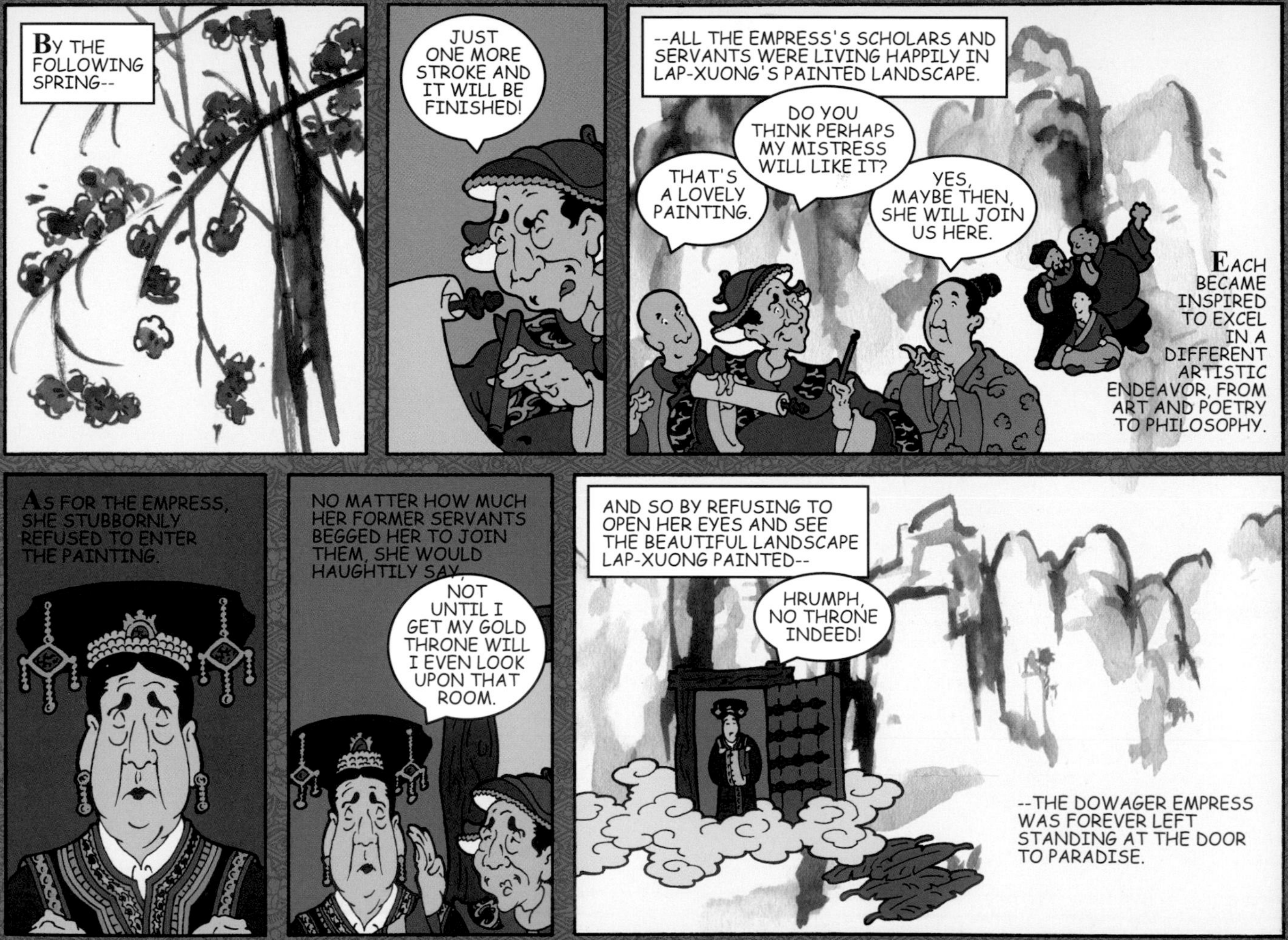
BY THE FOLLOWING SPRING--
JUST ONE MORE STROKE AND IT WILL BE FINISHED!
--ALL THE EMPRESS'S SCHOLARS AND SERVANTS WERE LIVING HAPPILY IN LAP-XUONG'S PAINTED LANDSCAPE.
THAT'S A LOVELY PAINTING.
DO YOU THINK PERHAPS MY MISTRESS WILL LIKE IT?
YES, MAYBE THEN, SHE WILL JOIN US HERE.
EACH BECAME INSPIRED TO EXCEL IN A DIFFERENT ARTISTIC ENDEAVOR, FROM ART AND POETRY TO PHILOSOPHY.
AS FOR THE EMPRESS, SHE STUBBORNLY REFUSED TO ENTER THE PAINTING.
NO MATTER HOW MUCH HER FORMER SERVANTS BEGGED HER TO JOIN THEM, SHE WOULD HAUGHTILY SAY,
NOT UNTIL I GET MY GOLD THRONE WILL I EVEN LOOK UPON THAT ROOM.
AND SO BY REFUSING TO OPEN HER EYES AND SEE THE BEAUTIFUL LANDSCAPE LAP-XUONG PAINTED--
HRUMPH, NO THRONE INDEED!
--THE DOWAGER EMPRESS WAS FOREVER LEFT STANDING AT THE DOOR TO PARADISE.

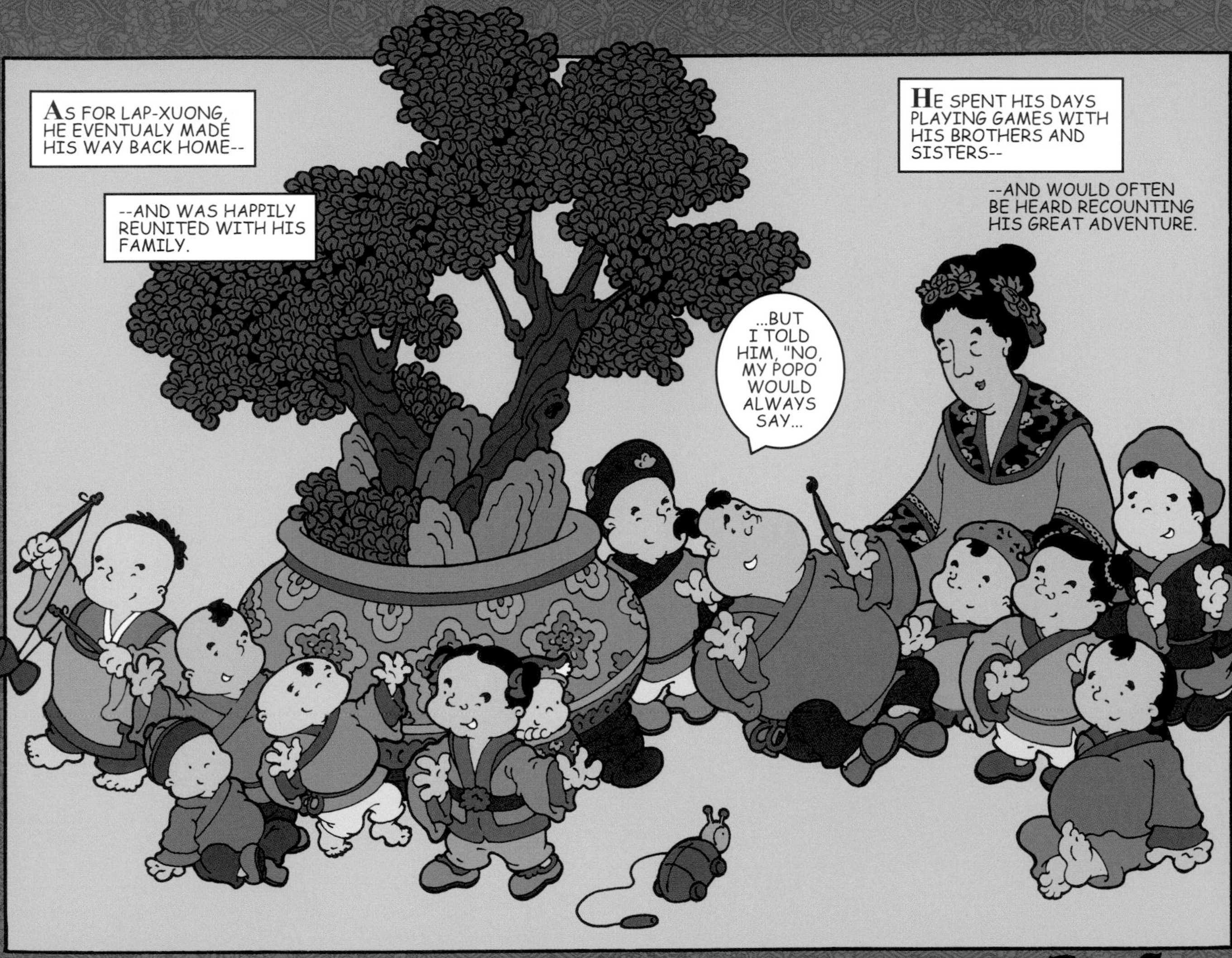
AS FOR LAP-XUONG, HE EVENTUALY MADE HIS WAY BACK HOME--
--AND WAS HAPPILY REUNITED WITH HIS FAMILY.
HE SPENT HIS DAYS PLAYING GAMES WITH HIS BROTHERS AND SISTERS--
--AND WOULD OFTEN BE HEARD RECOUNTING HIS GREAT ADVENTURE.
...BUT I TOLD HIM, "NO, MY POPO WOULD ALWAYS SAY...

THE END